JUST A MOMENT OF PEACE

MC. LAFAYETTE

© Copyright MCL Publishing

I pay tribute here to the elders of my family:

> To my great uncle Marcel,
> To my great aunt Louise,

And especially my grandmother, Françoise.

Some days, months, years are endless
Some minutes and seconds are a whole world

Jean d'Ormesson

JUST A MOMENT OF PEACE

Brussels 1958

Like every Sunday since the opening, Françoise and Louise come to Expo 58, The World Fair. There is everything, absolutely everything, in these northern districts of Brussels which cover dozens of square miles. The whole world has come together in their beloved city. You can taste all the cuisines of the world. You can drink all the exotic drinks. And, you can see all the planet does best and marvelously.

There are so many things to see that Françoise and Louise have decided to come every Sunday. Fortunately, admission is free.

Francoise and Louise are two sisters approaching their sixties. They are very close and enjoy their time together trying out new adventures. They have a good nature and are always ready to joke, tease and laugh. And, like many sisters, they bicker, too. To prepare for their outings to Expo 58, they take out their Sunday best dresses, shoes and hats. In fact, it's what everyone does. It's like going to a party! The men are all in suits with white shirts, dark ties, shined shoes and a Fedora to top it all off. The women don their most beautiful outfits – some very simple and others very sophisticated.

Ah! Expo 58! Everyone has been waiting for this event for so long. It has been 23 years since the World Fair has stopped in Belgium.

*

The first World Fair took place in London in 1851. Depending on the desires and ambitions of the hosting countries, this huge fair is held every three or four years and brings together the best of each participating country. For a few months, the host city becomes the center of the world and attracts millions of visitors.

Initially, the World Fair was, above all, a major technical and scientific showcase. Over the decades, the arts and lifestyles have been invited to these major international gatherings making them an even bigger and more popular celebration.

This was the fourth time since it began that Brussels hosted the World Fair. Construction and fitting-out work began in 1952, the exhibition was to open in 1955. But, due to political tensions of the Korean War, the opening was delayed. Finally, on April 17, 1958, the young King Baudouin officially opened Expo 58. It remained open until October and welcomed more than 40 million visitors. The event was the first major exhibition since the end of the WWII and the largest countries in the world participated to show their best.

The buildings and pavilion built for the occasion compete in originality and ingenuity. Reinforced concrete was invented and allows for construction never before imagined. Some of the structures still exist today like the Atomium. But, all the shops, bars and restaurants that were built to accommodate the millions of visitors have since disappeared.

At the heart of "The Glorious Thirties", the population slowly entered the consumer society and hoped to be at the dawn of a period of peace, prosperity and progress. The UN, NATO and the European community have just been created. Places where politicians can talk rather than go to war.

Sputnik travels through space and sends "beeps" back to Earth which greatly upsets the Americans. The rivalry in the conquest of space has just begun.

*

All of these considerations are superbly ignored by Françoise and Louise. They came to be entertained and to marvel at the sights. They look at the amazing newly constructed buildings, they listen to representatives of distant lands bragging about their climate, and they eat and drink some of the different cuisines from time to time. On a flyer distributed free to all visitors a small, barely noticeable, attraction will catch their attention.

More than a hundred film critics from all the participating countries are presenting

Battleship Potemkin which has been elected the best film of all time.

Since the end of WWII, Françoise and Louise have become avid movie lovers. It is especially on winter Sunday afternoons they go to the movies. So, when they learn the best film in the world is there in a theater just a few steps away, they rush like thousands of other curious people to the only cinema at Expo 58.

They sit in beautiful crimson red velvet armchairs. They bounce their butts in the seats and look at each other with a satisfied smile. The soft spring is very comfortable. It's definitely much better than the wooden chairs at the downtown theaters where they usually go.

The lights dim and the movie begins.

Françoise and Louise look at each other with a heavy sigh. The movie is not at all what they expected. It's a silent movie in black and white. The violins and trumpets in the background music are extremely loud. The title cards are in Russian with French subtitles. They are disappointed in the film, but, they stay. Luckily, the movie isn't very long... barely an hour.

When it is over, most of the audience come out of the theater dazzled by the flamboyance of Eisenstein, the director. Others, like Francoise and Louise, say nothing. They are already thinking about the next attraction they will attend hoping it will be more entertaining.

Next to the theater is a large café terrace with tables and chairs ... and there are seats available. Without saying a word, Françoise and Louise sit down and order two "Krieks", a sweet cherry-flavored beer.

Louise starts the conversation.

"I prefer movies with James Stewart..."
"And, I prefer color films..."
"The Hitchcock Movies..."
"Talking movies... where you don't have to read..."
"... or 'Singing in the Rain'... I've always loved this movie..."
"Maybe we just didn't understand anything."
"That must be it... we didn't understand anything."

"At least the chairs were comfortable."
"Oh, yes!"

A gentleman at the next table interrupts the conversation between Françoise and Louise.

"Excuse me, ladies, if I may."

Françoise and Louise nod and the man continues, "It's true the movie is a bit old. Especially if we compare it to today's films that are talking, in color, in cinemascope, and all the new inventions. But, this film is a testimony. It explains how the first world war began."

Louise asks, "In 1905?"

Françoise jumps in, "I thought it was the assassination at Sarajevo that started the war."

The man smiles and tips his hat a little. "Allow me to introduce myself. My name is Jean Dubois." Françoise and Louise smile and introduce themselves as well.

The man continues.

"The Sarajevo assassination is just the spark that ignited the barrels of gunpowder that had been accumulating for almost 10 years. The *Battleship Potemkin* retraces authentic facts that occurred in the port of Odessa in Russia. In June 1905, the mutiny on the ship begins. Why? Spoiled meat is served to sailors while the ship's officers receive fresh meat. It was a symbol of the Russian feudal society of the time. The mutiny swells and soon becomes an insurrection in the city.

This revolt, which will be violently and bloodily repressed, is the culmination of a series of other local revolts and street demonstrations throughout the country. All these events will lead to the promulgation of a new constitution and many reforms that really don't satisfy the Russian people.

To protect the state and its power, the Tsar increases the military budgets and the Russian armies become gigantic. This scared the Germans who followed in the footsteps of the Russians and rearmed heavily on land and sea. Seeing the development of the German fleet, England also launched a huge rearmament plan and France was not far behind.

In a few years, all of Europe is "armed to the hilt."

Françoise and Louise are all ears as they drink in the words of their personal speaker.

Jean Dubois continues.

"The politics become tangled, and Germany feels stuck between Russia and France. The Kaiser of Germany signed the Triple Alliance with Austria-Hungary and Italy. France, England and Russia are bound in the Triple Entente Treaty. So, here we are! Everything is in place for a great explosion. Everyone is armed. All that's missing is a little spark and it will happen soon. It will be Sarajevo."

Françoise and Louise, a little dazed, remain speechless through the story.

As usual, Louise is the one to start with questions. "How do you know all this?"

With a small smile, Jean Dubois gets up from the table and tips his hat again. "I am a history teacher. But, you know, not everyone agrees with me. Some say it's the defeat of

Russia against Japan in September 1905 that started the war. But I prefer my version. It's more poetic. Sorry to have disturbed you, ladies." And he leaves.

Françoise and Louise look at each other with wide eyes of surprise and also admiration of the gentleman's presentation.

Louise is the first to speak. "We really meet some interesting people here."

Francoise replies, "Yes, but maybe we should have listened more to our teachers at school."

Louise replies, "What are you talking about? We were out of school before the First World War started. Our teachers didn't have crystal balls to teach us about the future!"

Françoise and Louise laugh heartily.

After paying for their drinks, they go to the tram which will take them close to home. Once settled in, they think of Marcel and try to remember the stories he told them.

Marcel was their brother-in-law, the husband of their older sister, Jeanne. He was always eager to tell stories to his two young sisters-in-law who could not know, like life before World War I, in which he had served and the first industrial revolutions.

*

For several decades, the successive industrial revolutions had enriched a bourgeois class which had become dominant and the factories had emptied the countryside. Sharecroppers and small farmers had left for the big factories. The workers were paid a pittance for 80 hours of work per week. This meager salary was halved for women. Over the years and through the deplorable working conditions, the anger grew more and more.

Marcel said the big industrial bourgeoisie dreamed of a great conflict to extinguish workers' demands. The new industrial opportunity could be armaments. They would not only manufacture all the guns and all the artillery but also millions of bullets and shells.

*

Yes, Françoise and Louise remember all that very well. They were younger, but they also recall the carefree life he liked to describe before the First World War.

In Marcel's opinion, everyone was happy despite the harsh working conditions. New ideas and inventions kept coming including the first silent films, the first airplanes, and the first automobiles. Never had the world seemed so rich and happy. The energy of progress and its impact seemed inexhaustible. Why would it stop?

That's what Marcel thought. Little did he know what was coming.

*

Between the assassination of Sarajevo and the global intense reaction, there was the month of July 1914, and a few days in August, when the world changed forever.

Archduke Francois Ferdinand, heir to the Austro-Hungarian Empire, and his wife, were assassinated on June 28, 1914 in Sarajevo by Gabriel Principe, a Serbian nationalist. The Austrians considers this murder as an attack on the divine monarchy. The rest of the world perceives the event as a just another news item. No one cares about what's happening in the Balkans' powder keg.

For a long time, the Austrians have wanted to control Serbia and all the Slavs in the region, but the Balkans benefit from Russian protection. Nicolas II has been Tsar of all the Russians for thirty years. His dynasty has ruled the country for three centuries.

Three days after the assassination, in France, all military officers are called to duty. On July 23, 1914, the Austrians, with the approval of Kaiser Wilhelm II of Germany, issue an ultimatum to Serbia. They demand the Vienna police be allowed to investigate the murder in Sarajevo. Serbia refused.

Austria declares war on Serbia.

The world is suddenly afraid of war. US President Woodrow Wilson, in an official speech, confirms the neutrality of his country.

On July 28, 1914, Belgrade is bombed by the Austrians. In reaction,
the Russians, protectors of Serbia, amass soldiers on the Austro-Hungarian border.

On July 30, 1914, Wilhelm II sends an ultimatum to his cousin Nicolas II. "You must withdraw the Russian troops from the Austrian border".
Nicolas II's response is to send even more soldiers.

On August 1, 1914, Wilhelm II declared war on Russia and mobilized young Germans who were given the symbolic spiked helmets that were designed to protect them from saber blows. German soldiers are enthusiastic and ready to protect their country.

In Russia, Nicolas II, revered as a god, asks heaven for the protection of Holy Russia.

Rasputin, close to the Tsar and his family, begs Nicolas II not to go to war. "It will be the end of Holy Russia and the end of your reign." But, his pleas fall on deaf ears.

In France, Jean Jaurès, who is a left-wing politician and committed pacifist, asks all working forces in Europe to ignore the call of the armies. The next day, he is murdered.

In Paris, the French are focused on the "Tour de France". Ironically, this famous world race started on the same day of the assassination of François Ferdinand in Sarajevo. Time for a "Tour de France" and the world is turned upside down.

Throughout the country, the posters of the order for general mobilization are plastered in all the towns and villages. The French remain dumbfounded. All men between the ages of 20 and 48 must report for duty. Why? They are not at war.

But on August 3, 1914, Germany declared war on France who is an ally of Russia. The Germans kick-off Plan XVII. The objective is to invade France and conquer Paris.

The mobilization is now across Europe: 3 million French, 5 million Russians, 4 million Germans and 2 million Austrians.

After 50 years of peace on the European continent, none of these young men know what war is. They think of a heroic and masculine adventure. They believe in the defense of their country, and they are sure of an imminent victory which will be quick. No one doubts it.

Before the Russians were able to open a front in the East, the Germans invaded and occupied Belgium and Luxembourg to secure position to better attack France from the North.

On August 4, 1914, the front page headline of the major Brussels daily newspaper, "*Le Soir*", reads: "GERMANY VIOLATES BELGIAN NEUTRALITY."

Following the invasion of Belgian territory, England reacted immediately and declared war on Germany. But, the Germans were not too concerned. The English soldiers would not have time to land on the continent before the Belgian occupation was completed.

The Germans underestimated Albert I, the King of the Belgians who was a real soldier with a strong character. The military resistance organized by the King and his staff caused the Germans to lose many days. But the law of numbers plays against the Belgians and they have to back down. But, not without fighting and destroying their own railways to slow down the German armies.

Meanwhile in Serbia, the Austro-Hungarian soldiers who thought they would make short work of the Serbian soldiers got bogged down in the conflict and lost tens of thousands of men.

All this leaves time for England to mobilize and organize its naval force under the command of a certain Winston Churchill. Without compulsory military service, England must appeal to volunteers. And it works! In a few days, the English army went from 100,000 men to one million.

*

Louise remembers. "It was August 12, 1914. Marcel read about the King's acts of bravery every day in the newspaper. And, he made his decision."

"Yes, it was a fateful day that Marcel never forgot."

*

After a local victory for the Belgian army against the German soldiers, Marcel was convinced he had to commit himself to the King who was defending his country inch by inch and who was delaying the advance of the German troops as much as possible.

Marcel is a strong, natural born leader and he has no trouble convincing his friends to join the charge. He knows how to talk to them.

"It will just be a few weeks," he told them. "It's our duty. We have to go!"

He convinced three men from the workshop: Alphonse, whom everyone calls Fons because it's shorter; John, whom everyone calls Fat John because he's fat; and Isidore, whom everyone calls Isidore because he likes his first name.

The next day, Marcel and his three friends who have now become his companions in war are on the train heading for the main barracks in Antwerp. They are warmly welcomed and issued their uniforms and equipment. They change into their uniforms and familiarize themselves with their weapons. They've all done their mandatory two-year military service so there's not much to teach them.

A few days later, Marcel learns the Germans have bombed the historical monuments of Brussels and the small towns around the capital. The Kaiser's army has invaded Brussels. The other big cities of the country are besieged and fall one after the other. Massacres of civilian populations are on the rise. Marcel goes into a dark rage.

*

General Joffre of the French army asks King Albert I to hold back the 150,000 German soldiers around Antwerp to ease the pressure on his army in northern France. The mission will be accomplished thanks to the heavy artillery of the Belgian army. During this time, Marcel, his friends and all the other soldiers fall back towards the North Sea.

General Joffre orders a retreat of all allied forces on the Marne to build a continuous front line. King Albert I's army is called in as reinforcements to prevent a back-door attack. The French, English and Belgian stand firm and push back the German armies.

In September 1914, German submarines, called U-Boats, partially destroy the British fleet. On land, the German victories continue one by one, and they are now only 50 miles east of Paris.

Around Paris, German artillery resounds at every moment, day and night. Paris suffered its first aerial bombings but defended itself by all means - in the sky and on the ground.

To the north and east of the French capital, thousands work on the city's fortifications. Woe to the German airman who had to emergency land in the area. His execution is generally carried out immediately by the workers with their shovels, pickaxes and bare hands.

To the north of Paris, the French and the English push back the Germans and want to join the Belgian forces to form a single defense front. It's the race to the sea. It will be the last operation of mobile warfare.

The Belgian army strategically flooded the region of Ypres by opening the locks at high tide in the North Sea. The Yser River overflowed and created an almost impassable barrier three miles wide and one yard deep. The German artillery retreated. Mission accomplished!

The liaison between the allied armies is made. The race to the sea is a success. More than 600 miles of trenches from the North Sea to Switzerland form the strategic combat front between the Germans and all the allied forces. The war of movement has turned into a war of position.

By October 1914, only three months after the conflict started, the war has already caused more than two million deaths. The war has become an all offensive being fought on land, at sea and in the air. All of Europe is fire and blood.

And, it's just the beginning! Because of treaties, alliances and affinities, the war spread to all geographical areas of the planet including Africa, Asia, and South America. The conflict has become the First World War!

*

In the tram, Françoise and Louise continue their chatter and exchange of memories of the stories Marcel told them and try to put everything together.

Francoise says, "Perhaps we should have kept notebooks of the stories we heard from Marcel. It would be easier to remember."

"As tragic as some of the stories were, we probably never thought we'd want to remember them." replies Louise.

*

It's autumn in the trenches of northern France on the Belgian border. Marcel is languishing in a muddy trench. The Yser river is no longer wide enough at this point and they had to dig ... quickly.

Nobody, including Marcel, knows yet the conflict has become a war of position. He continues to dig deeper and deeper trenches. He doesn't want to bend over all the time to avoid German bullets. Isidore, Fat John and Fons, his neighbors in the trenches, do the same.

But the trenches are still not deep enough. They regularly hear the German bullets whistling overhead. You have to be careful. So, they continue to dig well into the night until they collapse from exhaustion. Tomorrow, they will start again.

During the night, guard duty tours are organized. Every hour, the guard soldiers are relieved and they go to sit in the trench where they sometimes fall asleep. Occasionally, a few sniper bullets whistle overhead.

The night is dangerous. Everyone stays on the lookout.

The daily work of the soldiers is repetitive - digging the earth, building a low, protective wall with sandbags and reinforcing their trenches with large tree branches.

Days, nights and weeks go by and it's almost the end of autumn. It has started to get cold. The rain turns the ground into sticky mud and the cold freezes the fingers. The trenches are now deep. There are even rear trenches to safely get to the small areas in the back to get food and rest -only with the permission from an officer.

Hundreds of wood planks are delivered in Marcel's trenches. They are thrown on the ground like a makeshift parquet floor. It's ugly, but no one cares. At least you don't have to walk in the mud anymore.

As he faces the German trenches, there are Belgian soldiers and the Scottish reinforcements to the left of Marcel, and to the right are the French soldiers. They all dig and deposit the dirt in front of their trench to build a protective barrier and reinforce the sandbags already there.

Over time, little by little, the miserable life of the soldiers becomes organized. But, it is organized in ignorance. No one knows why everyone is fighting. There is talk of an Austrian prince assassinated in Serbia and of Germans invading other countries, but Marcel doesn't understand any of it. He decides to write notes in his little notebook to keep track of information and ideas as they come to him. He always has a small notebook with him along with a pencil he regularly sharpens.

Today, he posts in his notebook, "I'm a little angry with myself for having brought three of my friends into this mess. Everyone believed it would be a short war. Everyone was wrong, I think."

There is now a daily routine of chores. Cleaning latrines, filling and repairing sandbags, reinforcing wooden structures, checking weapons and bullets. You have to fire five bullets a day at the enemy trenches and try to hit a German soldier… day and night. The Germans are doing the same.

Barely 100 yards separate the German and allied trenches, sometimes less. This space between is known as "no man's land" and the soldiers protect it like it's their most valuable possession.

In the tumult and troop movements, Marcel and his friends no longer know exactly where they are. They know the border is not far. But on which side?

Marcel finds the time long, very long and cold and damp. Tarps and blankets are waterlogged. He sleeps sitting in a hole he dug in the wall of the trench next to his post. His three friends from the workshop do the same or stand guard. Every three hours, it's his turn to put his rifle between the sandbags and observe the enemy trench.

Marcel laughs as he sees the tops of the spiked helmets sticking out of the German trenches. They make a very good target. It's almost like the carnival shooting galleries at the *Foire du Midi* fair. When an officer asks him if he has fired his five bullets, that's what he does. He shoots the tip of the German helmet. Everyone hears the metallic ping and laughs. Except the Germans. For a few hours, you no longer see the points of helmets sticking out above the trenches.

It is with a smile that Marcel notes this little anecdote in his notebook.

At the end of 1914, the landscapes were still somewhat civilized. In the distance, there are meadows and beautiful brick farmhouses. There are colors all around the trenches - the brilliant green of the grass, the golden yellow of the wheat fields and the crimson red of the roofs which have survived three months of conflict.

In mid-December, the colors slowly fade and a white blanket of snow begins to cover the plain. With the snow comes the cold and everyone grumbles at the discomfort of the freezing temperatures. Extra blankets are handed out and soups are boiled in the rear kitchens in hopes it will at least be lukewarm by the time it reaches the soldiers' mouths.

Marcel is sitting with his friends Fons, Isidore and Fat John in the trench by the brazier, a portable heater made of a pan with lighted coals. Fons is next to him. Fons is always next to Marcel. Fons is small, weak, and fearful, and he compensates by being a little mean. He barks often, but never bites. He listens to everything, but says nothing. He waits for Marcel to speak to agree with him. This annoys Marcel. But he doesn't say anything. He feels responsible. It's partly because of him that Fons is in the trenches.

Fons is a redhead and not very smart. Men don't like redheads; they have a bad reputation. Women do not find him attractive; he is too small. Fons is not yet 25 years old and he has already lost his parents. They drowned in a river while trying to cool off on a hot Sunday afternoon. Marcel is an orphan, too. They realized this common point while having a drink at the bar after work one day and it brought them together. Fons is happy to have found a friend.

Isidore is not a very common name, but Isidore likes it. And, beware to anyone who would call him otherwise. Marcel thinks he should call him "Mustache" because of his thick and messy mustache. Isidore doesn't care if others don't like his moustache. He wears it to hide his missing teeth.

After he and his wife, Dorine, have four daughters, Isidore decided to stop having children. That's enough mouths to feed and he doesn't have an orchard where money grows on the trees. He regrets not having a son; but he loves his family. Isidore and Dorine get along like thieves at fairs. In fact, their relationship is so strong that some call them the "Isidorine". Isidore knows it is all in good fun, and he tolerates this butchering of his name. It's the only one, though.

Fat John has earned his name. He is fat. It's undeniable. He is a pastry chef in love with his job. He grew up in his parents' pastry shop and always enjoyed all the good sweet things that were never forbidden and always offered to him. He was never skinny. He grew up in the carelessness of sugar but he was not afraid of hard work. Since he was 14, he was in the kitchen at 2 a.m. When he was 16, he added a job at the Atelier St. Amand chocolate factory where he met Marcel.

At 18, he fell in love with Agnès, the butcher's daughter. Agnès is also plump for the same reasons as Fat John. Her parents never refuse her anything. On their first date, Fat John took Agnès on a ride on the city lake in a pretty white boat. He teased and joked about how they could make a perfect life together. "We almost have a full meal. You bring the meat. And, I'll bring the desserts. All that's missing are the vegetables." Agnès laughed and added, "Our kids will be grocers. That way, we'll have a full menu." They laughed together even harder.

Over the course of their time together, Fat John and Agnès continue to laugh and have fun. But then, after a short six month courtship, Fat John is off to war.

Marcel says to his friends around the brazier, "Guys, we have to find things to do. If we don't die from a bullet, we will die of boredom."

"Or cold." replies Isidore.
"Maybe, but the cold only lasts one season."

Everyone is in agreement. "Yes, but what can we do?"
"We'll see. We have to be on the lookout." replies Marcel.

*

Louise has drifted off into a nightmarish daydream of what the soldiers endured. She's interrupted by Francoise's question.

"Did you ever meet any of Marcel's friends?"

"No. But he often talked about them."

Marcel was much older than Françoise and Louise and he is no longer of this world [1]. All that remains are the little notebooks that

---
[1] see "The Kiss of the Rat"

Louise likes to browse when she is at her older sister's house.

Louise takes her embroidered handkerchief to wipe away tears that have come to her eyes. After a few minutes, she picks up the thread of stories of Marcel. Françoise fills in with details she remembers.

*

One morning, Sergeant Bonmariage arrives in the trench. He has a mission for a soldier. The captain of the company needs a courier. A guy who goes from trench to trench to pass the messages between the general staff. Marcel pushes Fons forward. The officer looks at Fons and Fons looks at Marcel. Marcel gives him a discreet and affirmative sign – go ahead. Fons agrees.

Sergeant Bonmariage says to Fons, " 2 p.m., trench 303, captain's shelter." And he leaves.

Fons looks at Marcel with a thousand questions in his eyes. Marcel takes his arm and leads him aside.

"Listen to me, Fons. Do you understand anything about this war? No? Me, neither. So, here's what you're going to do. Whenever you're in contact with officers, you open your ears and you listen to everything. And, when they ask you if you speak French, you say no. That way they will speak freely. Try to remember everything you hear. Then, when we are together again, we'll discuss it. Okay?"

Fons doesn't have it all figured out, but he agrees.

"Besides, that will give you something to do, right?" Marcel insists.

Fons nods in agreement.

Five minutes before 2 p.m., Fons finds himself in trench 303. He is looking for the captain, but it is the captain who finds him.

"Are you the new courier?"
"Yes," answers Fons.
"Come to my shelter. It will be quieter."

Protected from the artillery shells, the shelter is almost luxurious. It's dry and there is a brazier. In the middle, there is a table and four chairs. Fons would like to sit down, but no one invites him to do so.

The captain addresses his aide-de-camp and gives him orders to prepare the papers. He turns to Fons and asks, "Do you know the numbers of the trenches?"

Fons shakes his head.

The captain continues, "All the 100 trenches are the first in the front line. The 200 are the second and the 300 are the third. And between these lines of trenches, there are small trenches that connect them. Easy, right?"

Fons nods and receives an envelope to deliver to Captain Labrosse of the second French regiment in trench 354. Fons leaves to navigate the trenches.

After walking for two hours, he finally arrives and gives the big envelope to Captain Labrosse taking care to give him the proper military salute.

The captain opens the envelope and reads. He smiles, he grunts, he sometimes seems surprised.... He turns to his two lieutenants and begins to speak, "Here is the news from our Belgian friends..."

Just then, one of his lieutenants nods toward Fons to remind the captain he is there. The captain turns to Fons whose has not yet spoken and asks him, "You speak French?"

Fons doesn't say anything, doesn't move and just makes a little ignorant face.

"Very well!" and he turns to his officers.

"Do they only have Flemish in the Belgian army?"

Everyone laughs heartily, except Fons, who is not supposed to have understood. But he absorbs every word.

After long discussions, Fons is given another large envelope which he will bring back to his captain.

After another two hours of walking in the cold and under the whistling of bullets, he delivered the envelope to his captain and was released from his responsibilities until tomorrow. He goes in the direction of his trench and meets Sergeant Bonmariage.

"All is well, Soldier Fons?"
"Yes, Sergeant. It's okay."
"Mission accomplished?"
"Mission accomplished!"
"Very well. Go and rest."

Sergeant Bonmariage comes from a family of soldiers. The values of military courage and discipline have been taught to him since childhood. He would like to be a hero and become an officer. But he is a little disappointed by the turn this war is taking and by the butchery of the first months. He remains patient. Things can change. In the meantime, he takes care of the men of his platoon. All the soldiers have been assigned service numbers, but he refuses to call them by their numbers like the other sergeants. Sergeant Bonmariage has memorized all the first names of his soldiers – all 32 of them. Three months ago, there were 50.

A few minutes later, Fons finds Marcel. He collapses next to his friend in a hole dug in the wall of the trench. It's already evening. Marcel and Fons are waiting for soup while drinking cold coffee. Isidore and Fat John join them.

Marcel begins to speak,

"So, how was your walk?"
"Cold! With the bullets overhead and the snow underfoot."
"Did you learn anything?"
"Not sure. I don't understand all this military gibberish. But apparently they won't attack right away."
"That's good."

Marcel continues.

"They know you speak French?"
"No, I played dumb."
"I'm sure you did it very well."

Fons shrugs and Marcel smiles at his little joke. Fat John and Isidore laugh heartily.

"Come on Fons, it's just a joke. Tell me, how are the trenches over there?"

"It's like here. Dirty and smelly. And there are rats like here. But there is something that really surprised me. First, the French soldiers have red pants. But above all, they don't have helmets!

Marcel can't believe it and Fons continues.

"It seems they will soon receive their helmets. But still. When you go to war, you have to provide the proper equipment. Otherwise, it's a butcher's shop."

Marcel reflects.

"We have the equipment and it's still the butcher's shop."

Marcel is telling the truth. In the trenches around him he saw at least a quarter of the soldiers dead or seriously wounded beyond return. He doesn't know the true casualty totals yet, but he figures he's lucky. He and his friends are still alive.

That evening, Marcel posts in his notebook: "First mission of the courier Fons - The

French soldiers have red pants and no helmets."

During the day, like everyone else, Marcel repairs and reinforces his trench. He still fires five rounds a day. He also tries to improve his comfort a bit. During the night, he falls asleep sitting up stupefied with fatigue. He is never far from the brazier. And, Fons continues his walks through the allied trenches.

One night, while standing guard, Marcel stares out between the sandbags at "no man's land." He asks himself a thousand questions and he has no answers. He feels within himself the anger of ignorance and uselessness.

To calm himself down, he thinks of the Saturday evening dance halls and the young girls he loved to hug during the java's, and the nights which were not always lonely.

He longs for the small chocolate workshop where he takes care of machine maintenance. Even if he dreams of bigger and better opportunities, he loves his job. The boss is nice and chocolate has always made him smile. When he talks about what he does in the workshop, people always ask him, "Do you like chocolate?" He always replies, "No, I *love* chocolate."

But all that is over now.

Since the start of the conflict, he has been a simple soldier under the high command of the King whom he has followed in all the battles. It was necessary, at all costs, to slow down the progression of the Germans and to defend the towns and the valleys inch by inch. Every mile counted, but there were too many soldiers on the enemy side. It was therefore necessary to retreat but still keep fighting.

After three months of conflict, like all the other soldiers, he dug a hole and the holes became trenches...deeper and deeper. This is where Marcel finds himself... his heart full of melancholy.

The next morning as the fine, icy snow continued to fall relentlessly, Marcel finished his coffee as Sergeant Bonmariage approached him.

"Good morning, Soldier Marcel."
"Good morning, Sergeant."
"I have a new job for you."
"Oh?"

"I saw you with your comrades. They listen to you. I really want to promote you to corporal. What do you say?"
"That's not a good idea, Sergeant."
"Why not?"
"Sergeant, I do not have the soul of a soldier and even less of a corporal. I simply followed our King to defend our country. And if my friends listen to me, it is because I am responsible for the maintenance of the machines in the workshop where we all work."
"I understand, soldier. But I'm disappointed."

After a few moments, Sergeant Bonmariage continues.

"So, If I need you in the back to fix something, can I count on you?"
"No problem, Sergeant."
"It's a deal."

"Sergeant, before you go?"
"Yes? "
"Could you do something for us? So we could clean up? Some hot water? Some soap? It's been over three months since we've had a bath."
"I'll see what I can do."
"Thank you, Sergeant."

Sergeant Bonmariage turns on his heels and leaves. He's a little disappointed. The promotion of Marcel would have allowed him to delegate some duties. Never mind, he'll find another soldier...one with the soul of a corporal. But first, he has to find basins, hot water and soap.

In the afternoon, Marcel writes everything down in his little notebook.

Fat John approaches Marcel and sits down next to him.

"Marcel, I have a favor to ask of you."
"Go ahead."
" Could you write me a nice letter for my little Agnès?"
"I never wrote a love letter, Fat John."

"But you can write. I see you writing in your notebook ... all the time."
"It's not the same thing."
"I know. But could you try? I know the words, but I can't put them to music. I'm sure you can."

Marcel looks at Fat John.

"Okay. Give me your lyrics and I'll add the music. We'll talk about it tonight, Fat John. Okay?"
"Thank you, Marcel."
"But you provide the paper, the postcards and the pencils!"
"Sure."

Fat John leaves almost cheerful and with a heart full of love for his future fiancée.

After Fat John leaves, Marcel is pensive. He has no one to whom he can write a love letter. Perhaps writing for Fat John will be good practice for the day when.......

After the evening grub, Marcel and Fat John sit down on a crude bench. The wood is dirty, but it's better than sitting in the mud. Fat John starts to speak but Marcel interrupts him.

"Have you seen Fons?"
"No, he's on a courier mission."
"And Isidore?"
"He's in the rear. Sergeant Bonmariage sent him over there."
"Good. Go ahead...tell me about Agnès."

Fat John takes a deep breath. "Agnès is adorable. She's plump like me and she laughs at all the nonsense I tell her. I'm the pastry chef's son and she's the butcher's daughter. On the third date, I kissed her on the mouth, and before leaving, I hugged her close. We get along very well and I love her big rosy cheeks."

Fat John stops, thinks a minute and finally concludes. "Voila!"

Marcel is a little appalled. "If I put your words to music, it will sound like a big fanfare with trumpets and drums."

Fat John wants to defend himself. "But..."

"Don't worry, Fat John. We'll figure it out."

Fat John is disappointed that Marcel does not share his enthusiasm for Agnès.

"Fat John, listen to me. A love letter is written with harps and violins not with a bass drum. You have to be light and at the same time sweep her off her feet. You have to convince her that you love her."

Fat John is a little confused. "And how do we do that?"

"Let me think about it. Tonight, I'll come up with something."
"Marcel, how do you know all this?"

Marcel looks Fat John in the eyes and pokes his friend's belly with his finger. "While you were eating pastries, I was reading."

Fat John smiles and Marcel writes down his first ideas.

About that time, Fons and Isidore come from behind.

Marcel greets them. "How are you, guys?"

Fons responds first. "I have big news. It seems the Germans are preparing convoys to bring heavy artillery into the area."

"Not good!" Marcel exclaims.
"But the big artillery shouldn't arrive until next year."
"That gives us time to prepare."
"And you, Isidore, what's up?"

"I became a gunner - machine gunner – with a half day of training. Aiming, shooting, loading ammo and cleaning. I'm ready to blast the spiked helmets."

The next morning, Isidore tries out his new weapon. There's no target in front of him. He just wants to shoot and brag to his friends, "I'm a real gunner now!"

Sergeant Bonmariage called him to order. "Save your ammunition, Soldier Isidore."

"Yes, Sergeant."

The sergeant turns to Marcel. "I need you in the rear, Soldier Marcel."
"Of course, Sergeant. I'm with you."

"And you, Soldier Fons. Go see if the captain needs you."

All day, Fat John and Isidore remain in the trench waiting and keeping watch, hoping that no German will target them. Between the boredom and the anguish of death, the day is unending. Isidore sits near his machine gun and keeps his hand on his new weapon and Fat John does nothing. He doesn't want to do anything. He thinks of Agnès, he thinks of his parents, he thinks of the good cakes from the pastry shop. He watches the snowflakes fall.

At the end of the day, the gang of four is together again. No one has anything to say. They eat in silence. Everything seems to fall on their shoulders - the snow, the night, the boredom and the fear of dying.

They organize the guard tours for the night. Isidore takes the first round from 10 p.m. to midnight. Then it will be Marcel.

The first shift is calm and at midnight, Isidore wakes up Marcel who joins him at the guard post hidden behind the sandbags.

"Everything went well?" Marcel asks.
"Everything is calm. Guess they're all sleeping on the other side."

Marcel sneers, "I doubt that."

Suddenly, Marcel and Isidore hear a steeple bell. The church must be far away. The sound is weak, but continuous. For several minutes, the three bells ring. Their trench comrades wake up and come to listen to the music of the bells. They finally understand. It's Christmas! They start to smile. Some look at the stars in the dark night and then back at the misery of their trench.

Without particular enthusiasm, the soldiers wish each other "Merry Christmas". A few hug each other. The soldiers smile at their companions in misfortune. Sergeant Bonmariage arrives and takes out a bottle of whiskey and orders all the soldiers, "Raise your glasses!" Everyone laughs and presents their metal cups. The sergeant pours a shot of whiskey into the cups. The soldiers clink their cups and take a drink. Some of the soldiers are still laughing.

A soldier goes between trenches 200 and 300 and pulls out one of the last remaining bushes. Back in the first trench, he collects some candles from the other soldiers, prunes the bush to make a small Christmas tree, and lights the candles.

"Here you go! It's Christmas!" says Marcel.

A sad smile freezes on the dirty faces of the soldiers. No one had imagined spending Christmas here. They all make a secret wish this will be their last Christmas in the trenches.

After a moment, a few empty cups clink together.

"Sergeant, that sounds empty!" Marcel exclaims.

The sergeant turns around.

"Careful, guys. Don't get drunk. There are those across from us who don't like us very much. We have to be able to aim straight all night."

Marcel, suddenly worried, climbs the first steps of his ladder of his guard post to see what's happening on "no man's land". He can't believe his eyes and calls to his superior.

"Sergeant Bonmariage, come and see."

The sergeant climbs one of the ladders and sees the spectacle on the other side of "no man's land". Among the Germans are dozens of small Christmas trees with dozens of small candles stuck between sandbags.

As far as he and Marcel can see along the enemy trenches, there are little trees or little bushes. Candles are burning all around.

Marcel can't help himself. "It's beautiful!"

Sergeant Bonmariage replies. "It's Christmas for everyone!" He turns to the soldiers in his trench. "Hand me the Christmas tree and the candles."

He spreads a few sandbags, pushes the small Christmas tree out on the ground and puts the candles around it. Soon, in the nearby trenches, all the soldiers are doing the same thing. The French, English and Belgians proudly brandish their little bushes surrounded by candles. The sight is luminous and magical.

All the soldiers stand on stools and benches or the first steps of the trench ladders to admire the flickering little lights.

Suddenly, the German soldiers are singing.

*Stille Nacaht! Heilige Nacht!
Alles schläft; einsam wachtnur das traute heilige Paar.Holder Knab' im lockigten Haar, sch lafe in himmlischer Ruh!*

Everyone listens to the Germans' Christmas carol. They don't understand the words they're singing, but they all recognize the tune – *"Silent Night"*.

When the German song ends, no one moves, no one speaks. Suddenly, the same Christian song begins to resound from the allied trenches :

Silent night, Holy night,
All is calm, All is bright
'Round yon Virgin, Mother and Child
Holy Infant so tender and mild
Sleep in Heavenly peace
Sleep in Heavenly peace

During the song, white flags are planted between the sandbags everywhere. They are handkerchiefs hung on a piece of wood. Everyone understands. We make a truce.

Coming from afar, everyone hears the beginning of a prayer, a prayer in Latin, the universal language of Christianity.

...
Seu stella partum Virginis Coelo micans signaveris, et hac adoratum die præsepe Magos duxeris.
Vel hydriis plenis aqua vini saporem infuderis: hausit minister conscius quod ipse non impleverat.
Gloria tibi, Domine, qui appearedisti hodie, cum Patre et Sancto Spiritu, in sempiterna secula.
Amen.

Either that You announce in Heaven the birth of the Virgin by a sparkling star, and on this Day lead the Magi to the manger, to adore You;
Either You give the flavor of wine to the amphorae filled with water, and make the servant taste the liquor that he had not poured there.
Glory to You, O Lord! Who appeared today; glory to You with the Father and the divine Spirit, forever and ever.
Amen .

"*Who is this man of faith lost among us?*" wonders Marcel.

Isidore knelt on a wooden plank with his face against the wall. Sometimes he raises his eyes and palms to the heavens with praise. Marcel is astonished as he watches Isidore in the simplest exercise of his faith - praying.

Fons and Fat John are sitting on a rudimentary wooden bench. They have their heads bowed as a sign of respect.

In the distance, soldiers, both enemies and allies, cautiously emerge from the trenches and find themselves in the "no man's land". They talk, shake hands, share the booze and clink glasses. Marcel and his friends still hidden in their trench watch this improbable sight.

Fons asks the question. "Are we going?"

The others are ready to go. Everyone except Marcel.

"I'm not going, but go if you want."

Sergeant Bonmariage overheard Marcel's remark. "You don't want to make peace, Soldier Marcel?"

"It's not peace. It's just a truce - a Christmas truce."

Marcel pauses a few seconds and then continues.

"Those "on the other side" are the ones who invaded my country, who brought it to its knees, who massacred civilians. So, it's a ceasefire. I will stop shooting, but that's all."

"That's reasonable, Soldier Marcel. Those who want to walk in the "no man's land" can go there."

A few soldiers, along with Isidore, Fat John and Fons but not Marcel, climb the ladders and come out of the trenches. They move timidly into "no man's land". They all kept their rifles with the strap hanging over the shoulder and the butts up.

From a distance, they begin to greet the Germans. First, a simple little wave of the hand. Then, the handshake and eventually, the whiskey. They try, with great difficulty, to talk to each other.

For a few hours, there are soldiers from both fronts in the "no man's land". From his trench, Marcel writes down everything in his notebook.

In the distance, a shot rang out. Everyone turns towards the source of the noise, but nothing happens. Maybe it's just a warning - the end of playtime. The soldiers slowly return to their respective trenches. Before descending back into the trenches, they turn to wave a last Christmas greeting to each other.

Isidore is the first to come back into the trench. He sees Marcel taking notes and says to him, "Bah! They're not bad guys. They're like us. They obey orders."

Marcel replies, "Yes, and tomorrow they will have orders to kill us."

End of the conversation.

Everyone settles down to sleep for a few hours. With bellies full of alcohol, sleep will be heavy.

The next morning, the white flags are still planted in the sandbags. It is December 25, 1914. The Christmas truce.

After noting a few more details in his notebook, Marcel begins to write for Fat John who has come to sit next to him.

The men of the canteen arrive in the trench with a large covered pot. The soldiers curiously approach. When the soldiers release the lid, a delicious smell of hot chocolate invades the trenches and the noses.

Everyone takes out their cup and waits their turn. The cups fill up quickly and the soldiers go back to their spots to enjoy the incredible luxury of hot chocolate.

More than any other, Marcel is over the moon. The most beautiful chocolate memories come back to him. He takes small sips so he can prolong the pleasure.

Sergeant Bonmariage arrives in the trench.

"Merry Christmas to all my soldiers!"
"Merry Christmas, Sergeant."
"I have a surprise for you!"

He turns around and motions for the nurse and orderlies to approach. They bring large white enamel basins, huge jugs of hot water, soap and towels.

"Don't fight. Get organized and take advantage since the bullets aren't flying over our heads."

The sergeant leaves with the orderlies and returns a few minutes later with new uniforms, new boots, clean belts and shiny buckles.

The reception given to the sergeant and to the men with laden arms is ecstatic.

"For the Sergeant: Hip Hip…"
"Hurrah"… yells everyone in chorus.

Three times in a row, Sergeant Bonmariage is cheered.

With a teasing air, he said to his men, "And I have sizes to fit each of you."

A few cries still echo in the trench as the sergeant goes back with his team to return with more large jugs of hot water.

The nurses, who have less work since the shooting has stopped, set up the five beautiful white basins on wooden planks along the walls of the trench. Towels and soap are placed between the basins. The water, clean and steaming, is poured and the first wave of soldiers begin to undress to the waist.

Some shiver from the cold, but they get used to it quickly.

They take off their pants and soap the happy parts. Next comes the feet. They really need it.

The water in the five basins is continuously changed with clean hot water to replace the sewage with the filth of the soldiers. The black waters are thrown over the sandbags into the "no man's land".

As soon as a soldier is clean, he lines up to receive his new uniform, his underclothes, his new boots and his belt. Before getting fully dressed, some shave. They want to indulge in every moment of feeling clean and handsome and….human…again.

The trench emanates a particular vapor and a peculiar smell - a mixture of soap and muddy grime never smelled before.

After an hour of warm and joyful washing, almost everyone sighs with pleasure. Only Fat John did not go to the basin.

Marcel asks him, "Well then, Fat John, you don't like soap?"

Fat John grimaces and Marcel comes and sits down next to him.

"What's the matter?"
"They're going to laugh at me and my big belly."

Marcel reflects.

"Go last. Fons, Isidore and I will hide you. Okay?"
"Okay."

And so it is done. Fat John's three friends stand together as a human shield to allow their friend to be naked and not have to suffer the mockery of others.

Faced with the ridiculousness of the situation, Marcel said to Fat John.
"Scrub well everywhere! You're the last one who doesn't smell of soap!"

The makeshift screen shakes with laughter.

"Don't worry, guys. I'm scrubbing."

*

Françoise and Louise burst out laughing in the tram.

"I would have liked to have seen that!" said Louise.
"Me too. But only on that day. This Christmas Day of 1914."
"Oh yes. The poor guys, they didn't know yet they were going to stay in their hole for several more years."

"When did Marcel realize that it was going to last much longer?"
"I don't know. Much later, probably. You have to keep hope. Until one day, you just give up, I guess."
"Poor Marcel, he didn't have much luck in his life."
"Oh! What do you mean? He met our sister."

Françoise and Louise smile at each other remembering the love Marcel and Jeanne shared. These memories are much better than the war stories they are now trying to put together.

*

After the bathing is finished and the new clothes are on, the remaining vapors of the hot water are now mixed with tobacco smoke and sighs of contentment. Most of the soldiers are quiet, lost in dreams of Christmas at home with family and loved ones. Some continue to polish themselves by cutting their nails and trimming their mustaches.

They are shocked by the hot water and the filth they have peeled off their bodies. Their clean skin makes them feel almost vulnerable as if they were naked. They had grown accustomed to their filthy, stinking bodies and their muddy, battered uniforms. It's almost like a new life is starting. But, they are still in their trench mired in conflict for no apparent reason. Fortunately, the white flags are still planted in the sandbags and provide a symbolic protection against the otherwise barbarism.

The next day, Fons must leave on a messenger mission. When he returns to his friends, he cannot hold himself back. He must tell them.

"The news isn't good, guys."

The three friends move closer to Fons.

"The officers are upset. They didn't like us making friends - friends with the spiked helmets."
"Is there going to be retaliation?" Marcel asks.
"Yes." replies Fons. "They're going to move troops to the Eastern Front."
"Should we be concerned?" Fat John asks.

"No. Apparently others did a lot more than us. Some played football, others got downright drunk with the Germans. It even seems that a German sang opera... in the middle of the "no man's land."

"It's going to heat up. There's no doubt about it." says Marcel.

Marcel climbs a ladder to look on the other side. The white flags are still there and the little Christmas trees, too.

He comes down and turns to his friends.

"Apparently the truce is not over yet."

Everyone smiles.

"Maybe it will last until New Year's Eve."
"Let's hope so."

For the next few days, the soldiers do not fire. They stroll, walk, talk to each other, warm up around the brazier, play cards. Life would be almost good if it weren't so cold.

Marcel has just finished the draft of his first love letter and calls Fat John.

"Fat John, I'm going to read you my draft letter. If you like it, you'll copy it in your own handwriting."

"Thank you, Marcel!"

"Don't thank me yet. You may not like it."
"I'm sure it will be very good."

Marcel begins to read.

My beloved, My Agnès,

Despite the tender and sweet memories, I still and always feel too far from you for too long. I remember your hands, your heart, your body. All I have are memories swirling around in my head.

I keep your portrait in my pocket near my heart. It reassures me and protects me. I really need it in this hell. Tomorrow, I will try, once again, not to die.

My beauty, I send you kisses and make you a promise. I'll be back soon to put my lips on yours. Do not forget me. I will never forget you.

Your John

As Marcel finishes reading, he looks at Fat John and sees he is moved by his words...with tears in his eyes.

"Do you like it, Fat John?"

"It's wonderful! I'm sure Agnès will love it. If after that she doesn't want to marry me, it's hopeless."

"She'll marry you, Fat John. Don't worry. But there are two conditions – that the war is over and that you are still alive."

Fat John takes the draft and leaves to copy it in his best handwriting. An hour later, he comes back to Marcel and gives him his draft. Marcel is surprised and Fat John says to him, "Keep the draft. Perhaps it will be useful to you some day." Marcel grins and puts the paper in his pocket. Marcel does not yet know that he will draft many more love letters for Fat John.

It is under the shelter of the white flags that the year 1914 will end- the first year of the First World War.

On January 2, 1915, things will change.

Behind the German trenches, incessant troop movements take place. Trucks come and go. And the white flags are gone.

Marcel is on the lookout. "The truce is over, guys. We're going to shoot again."

A few minutes later, Sergeant Bonmariage arrives in the trench and gathers his 32 men.

"Soldiers, listen to me. The fraternization is over. The war resumes. The King orders us to defend our positions. No matter what! We will not attack. We will defend. The mission will not be easy. The Germans will attack and try to destroy us by all means with their big guns and foot soldiers with rifles.

So, we have to prepare. We are going to receive hundreds of rolls of barbed wire. At the back, they prepare small Saint Andrew crosses. It will be up to us to install all this on the "no man's land". This work will be done under cover of night to avoid getting shot. So, you will sleep during the day. Understood? Any questions?"

Nobody reacts.

"First operation: Remove the white flags and little candle-lit bushes."

The make-do Christmas trees are thrown into the braziers and the soldiers retrieve their white handkerchiefs. Within minutes, no trace of Christmas is visible in the trench. The truce is over. The soldiers settle back into their routines. War has reasserted itself. Soldiers man the guard towers and surveillance while the others sit in the trench waiting for their turns.

Soon dozens and dozens of barbed wire rolls with Saint Andrew crosses were laid in the trench. Everyone is waiting for the darkness and the return of the sergeant with their orders.

After the evening grub, Sergeant Bonmariage is ready get the mission started. For several minutes, he observes "no man's land" through his binoculars.

He goes back down into the trench and gives his orders.

"You are going to hook the ends of the barbed wire to the Saint Andrew crosses.

Then, you are going to form teams of three all along our trench. The best shooters will be between the sandbags. On my signal, a team of three will advance to "no man's land". Go as far as possible, up to 10 yards from the German line. You plant the first cross on the left, extend the roll of barbed wire and plant the second cross on the right. Then, come back! All of this will be done crawling on the ground in silence. Understood?"

There is silence in the ranks.

"Go! Form your teams!"

Fons, Isidore and Fat John form a team of three. Marcel is their shooter. He's the best for the job.

The whole platoon seems ready. Every five yards, a team of three soldiers with a roll of barbed wire are ready to go out. Every ten yards a soldier with his rifle aimed is ready to fire on the German trenches.

"Soldiers! Jump up and down! If you hear metallic noises, empty your pockets."

Everyone hops around and removes the bowls, cups, spoons and coins before leaving the trench. Every soldier in the trenches always keep all their things on them. You never know when you will need them.

In the middle of the line of soldiers, the sergeant selects the first team.
"Go ahead! And be quiet! Shooters, get ready!"

The first team climbs out of the trench and crawls for several yards through the "no man's land" toward the German trenches. Cover shooters are on the prowl. Every five minutes, a new team is sent.

Five hours later, all the barbed wire is up and everyone is back.

"Mission accomplished, my soldiers. Congratulations! At dawn, we'll see what it looks like. Now, go and rest."

All the soldiers go back to their holes where they will sleep sitting up. Soon, the sun rises. The sergeant uses his binoculars to inspect the field of barbed wire on the "no man's land". He is satisfied.

"Good job, soldiers. We're gonna WIN this war."

Everyone quickly observes the results of their night work and congratulates each other. They feel somewhat protected.

From the German line came cries, protests and orders. The sergeant begins to laugh. "The spiked helmets are not happy. We were faster than them."

One morning, about a week later, the soldiers discovered barbed wire near the German trenches. The "no man's land" has become impassable.

*

Françoise asks Louise, "When did the first shells drop on them?"

"In January, but Marcel and his friends were prepared. Maybe that's what saved them."

"And to think, we were just young girls still at home and working on the farm at that time."

"Yes, and we were far from suspecting what was happening on the battlefields."

Françoise and Louise are thoughtful for a few seconds.

Louise breaks the silence, "And that was just the beginning."

*

In January 1915, the situation is calm and the soldiers have become accustomed to their little hell. They don't know yet that they are simply in purgatory. Hell is coming soon.

Every day, Fons gives Marcel, Isidore and Fat John news from his message deliveries. Artillery of all calibers is set up everywhere behind trenches 300.

Marcel is worried. "The shells are going to pass right over our heads."

Fons adds, "They had better aim well!"

"That's not what worries me." replies Marcel. "It's the German artillery. For them, we are the target. It won't take them weeks to adjust their guns and aim straight."

All four remain silent.

Isidore asks Marcel, "Do you have something in mind?"

Marcel looks at the trench, then at the sky, and then the trench again.

He turns to the others. "We have to start digging."

"But Marcel, it's useless. We can dig another 10 yards. The shells will just fall 10 yards lower," grumbles Fons.

"No, no. We're going to dig here." Marcel squats down and draws a rectangle showing 30 inches above the ground.

"We will dig a hole here - two yards long and 40 inches deep. As soon as there is an alert, we dive in and stay in the hole. The earth above us will protect us. When the shots stop, we come out and take aim to shoot at the Germans if they had the bad idea to try to get in our trenches."

Marcel stopped talking. He is quite happy with his plan. It's not perfect, but it's better than nothing. He turns to his friends. "So?"

Fons replies, "Okay! Well, we'll dig … Again!"

At the end of the day, four long holes behind the ladders are ready to accommodate four men. If there's an artillery alert, that's where they'll go.

Marcel feels good about the plan. He makes note of everything in his notebook.

They won't have to wait long for the baptism of fire. Two days later, the German artillery begins firing. Allied artillery, too. Shells are falling everywhere. The noise is deafening. Marcel and his friends are in their holes waiting for the shelling to end. Fat John has never been under fire. The only fire he knows is the one of his stove in the basement of the pastry shop. And it's the same for all the other soldiers. No one has ever experienced this intensity of attack and explosions.

After fifteen minutes of constant bombardment, the firing stops. The four friends come out of their holes and climb the ladder to the surface to observe the "no man's land". Their rifles are in aim, ready to fire, but nothing moves. The "no man's land" is full of shell holes and the barbed wires have suffered. Tonight, it will have to be repaired.

They look back to the trench and see several bleeding soldiers.
Those not injured help the wounded. So far, no one has died.

Sergeant Bonmariage inspects the trench and his men. Marcel stops him.

"Sergeant, look what we dug."

The sergeants kneels to get a better look at the holes.

As he gets up, he says, "Good idea, soldier. But who was on guard?"

"Not us, Sergeant."

"We will have to get that organized."

The sergeant calls all his soldiers to come to see Marcel's holes.

"Each man will dig his hole. Go!"

Marcel and his friends lend a hand to help each of the soldiers. One of the soldiers suggests calling the holes "Marcel holes". Everybody laughs, but also thinks it's a good idea. From then on, when shots begin, everyone dives into their "Marcels' holes".

The holes are completed just before the evening rations. Afterward, the barbed wire repair is done.

That evening, a few soldiers will be assigned additional work - construction of a special guard post protected from the bombardments and from where all of the "no man's land" can be watched in front of Sergeant Bonmariage's trench. The post will be slightly advanced, a little circular and the top protected by planks of wood and sandbags because now the danger comes from the sky.

After the job is done, the sergeant turns to Marcel.

"This way, only one solider will be on watch duty. There will be less risk. At the slightest movement of troops in front, he will give the alert."

After a few hours of sleep, everything begins again. The infernal noise of shells, repairs, guard duty, five bullets a day, three skimpy meals, lukewarm coffee and, for a few days, whiskey. Some soldiers are concerned. They don't want to drink away their youth. The alcohol rations are a little too generous and are distributed in the morning.

The following days, the bombardments became more and more intensive and lasted longer and longer. A few soldiers cannot take it anymore and begin to cry. The shelling is incessant, deafening and deadly.

In March 1915, the inevitable happened. Three soldiers from Sergeant Bonmariage's platoon were killed by shrapnel. They were lying in the "Marcel's holes". Only their backs were visible and that's where the shrapnel landed.

The sergeant evaluates the current holes, then orders three soldiers to fetch long and wide wooden planks and place them under each "Marcel hole". Now, when the soldiers dive into their holes, all they have to do is grab the board and put it over themselves for more protection.

Just like that, the "Marcels' holes" become "coffin" holes. At least their backs will be protected...a little.

With the onset of spring comes the first rains. But, it's not just the water that falls from the sky. There are still artillery shells falling, and they create mud rain in the trenches dirtying everything in their path. Artillery attacks continue to intensify even more. Soldiers spend several hours a day in their "coffin" holes. Any hint of a smile has faded from their faces. The trenches have become real cesspools.

At the beginning of the summer, the Germans began to attack the allied trenches. Always at dawn. But, it did not go well for them. Their attempts only lasted a few days, and the soldiers held the trenches with their rifles and machine guns. Isidore is pleased with himself.

Marcel notes in his notebook, "*I must have killed a few Germans today. I am neither proud nor sad.*"

The nightly barbed wire repairs continue because the shells are falling every day. The sergeant encourages his soldiers.

"We must resist! Again and again! They will not advance any further. We're gonna WIN this war!"

The faces of the soldiers are dirty and tired. There is spite in the looks and fatalism in the bodies.

Marcel approaches the sergeant. "Sergeant, when is Christmas?"

"In six months, Soldier Marcel."

"Will we have to wait six months to wash again?"

"No. It seems that there will be special leaves given to us."

"That's good. But where will we go? The French can go home. The English, too. But Belgium is occupied. I would be very surprised if the Germans will let us go through to go home for a bath."

"We may have an opportunity, soon." smiled the sergeant.

"What?"

"A few months ago, the French started handing out leaves. There were quite a few deserters. Many were caught. They were sent to the firing squad. So, since then, they have been waiting to give new leaves."

"Firing squad, huh?"

"Yes."

After a few moments, the sergeant resumes.

"A few miles from here, out of range of the German guns, they are in the process of setting up a house which will become something like an inn or hotel with an infirmary. It can accommodate ten soldiers at the same time."

"Good. Good. When can we go?"

"In a few weeks. Two soldiers per platoon at a time. Three days and two nights. I'll let you know, Soldier Marcel."

Weeks feel like months, but finally it happened. Marcel and Fat John are walking towards the long-awaited rest and relaxation at the inn. After more than two hours of walking, they arrive at the guard post of the inn and show their permissions to the sergeant on duty. He opens the gate for them and points to the path to follow. They are almost there. And, they will not be disappointed.

The inn is a very big house painted in a greenish gray so as not to attract attention.

A large hedge, seven feet high, surrounds the property.

Inside, they are greeted by Lieutenant Beauséjour.

"Welcome, soldiers! We rest and recharge here. That's what it's made for. The beds are comfortable. The food is good, and we have big tubs and hot water. I suggest you start with the bath. The smell is quite unbearable."

Marcel responds, "Yes. The hotel where we were was not very comfortable."

The lieutenant smiles. "I know, soldier, but it's war. Nevertheless, The King wants to take care of his soldiers. So, take advantage of your three days."

He hands them two keys.

"Bedrooms are upstairs. Bathrooms downstairs."

"Thank you, Lieutenant," respond Marcel and Fat John in unison.

When Marcel finds his room, he says to himself *"The staff didn't take any shortcuts in preparing the rooms."* The room is not luxurious, but it is nice and well kept. The sheets are clean. There are even two paintings on the walls. Behind a screen, there is a small sink and a toilet. Marcel puts his hands on the bed and presses to check the comfort. Not bad...

Marcel undresses but keeps his underwear that is now brown from time, dirt and sweat. He goes down to the bathrooms. There are six large tubs - three on each side. They are separated by sliding curtains.

A nurse greets him. "Welcome. Which bathtub would you like ?"

"I'll take the one by the window."

The nurse runs the hot water and Marcel sits down on a wooden stool next to his tub. He watches the water flow...warm, beautiful, clean and in abundance.

When Marcel is alone in the bathroom, he takes off his underwear which falls to the ground in a dirty, shapeless mass. He slips into the hot water. He gives a long sigh of relief. With a smile on his face, he just sits in the water and takes in the pleasure it brings. After several minutes of soaking in the hot water, he washes himself with the big bar of soap provided.

Fat John enters the bathroom with the nurse. They head for the tub across from Marcel's.

"Oh, Fat John, you're going to enjoy it!"
"No doubt!"

After turning on the water for Fat John, the nurse approaches Marcel's bathtub.

"You can change the water, Monsieur Marcel. It's black."
"Ah, yes! Good idea. Thank you, miss..."
"Anna."

After Anna leaves, Fat John roars with pleasure in his hot tub. Marcel laughs when he sees his friend wading in his bathtub.

"Marcel, I could stay here until the end of the war."

"I know. Me too. But don't have any grand illusions, Fat John. We have to go back."

"I know, I know."

After three baths and more than an hour in the water, Marcel and Fat John dressed in large terrycloth robes to go back to their rooms.

"What time do we eat here, Marcel?"
"I don't know. We'll get dressed and then meet downstairs. Okay?"
"Okay."

When they return to their rooms, they find underclothes, trousers and a canvas shirt. Everything is clean and ironed. When they arrive downstairs, they are like new men. They see other soldiers seated in large comfortable armchairs having drinks.

Everyone is there - two officers, a few nurses and some soldiers. The nurses are dressed in all white with their hair pulled up in a twisted bun and a small cap. They all wear red lipstick. The soldiers on leave are casually dressed in different colored canvas shirts. Marcel and Fat John are welcomed with handshakes as introductions of the men, ranks and units are made. Germain, one of the soldiers, leads them to the bar. "Here is the bar! And, it's all you can drink! But don't overdo it. It would be a shame to get drunk and not remember your time here. We have all the spirits and a lot of beers in the ice. Help yourself!"

Marcel and Fat John are not accustomed to strong alcohol so they stick to beer. They sit in the large armchairs which are indeed very comfortable.

Marcel addresses Germain. "I have never seen such armchairs."

"A gift from the English. They call it a Chesterfield."

There are several sizes and different colors of leather - dark red, warm brown and shimmering black. But all the chairs have the same particular rounded shape with the armrests as high as the backrests.

Marcel, Fat John and Germain each settle into an armchair and start to talk. But after a little small talk, the only real discussion on everyone's mind inevitably arises. "When is the war going to end?"

All the soldiers try to answer this simple question without finding a single clue. The officers and nurses do not get involved in this conversation. Anyway, nobody knows, but it's all the soldiers talk about for the next hour.

A cook arrives in the living room and invites the soldiers to come into the dining room. There are four large round tables. Everyone finds a seat. At each table, there are soldiers on leave, the soldiers who work here and the nurses. Even Lieutenant Beauséjour and his officers share tables with soldiers. That doesn't happen often.

The kitchen staff brings in tureens of soup and large bottles of beer. Everything is set out on the tables for the soldiers to serve themselves. The soup is hot and the beer is cold. Sitting on a real chair at a table with a beautiful white tablecloth, real plates and real metal cutlery is almost unbelievable, and Marcel and Fat John are enjoying every moment as if they were back at home in their favorite restaurant. The other soldiers seem to do the same.

When the main course is served, all forms of surprise and delight are expressed. They laugh, they shout, they knock on the table, they pat each other on the shoulder. Large dishes of traditional Belgian stew made with beef and dark beer are placed on the tables accompanied with potatoes topped with parsley. For twenty minutes, an almost suspicious silence reigns in the dining room. No words are spoken, but there is plenty of noise. The clinking of cutlery on the plates, the noisy chewing and the sighs of contentment fill the room. In the end, all the large dishes and soldiers' plates are empty. Even the sauce on the plates has been wiped clean with bread.

When the cooks return to the dining room with dessert, all the soldiers rise for a standing ovation to applaud the kitchen staff. Then they quickly sit back at the table to effortlessly devour the vanilla caramel flan that had arrived at the tables.

With their bellies full, the soldiers return to the living room.

Germain approaches Marcel and Fat John.

"I recommend a sip of strong alcohol. You have to swallow it quickly. It will help with digestion."

Marcel is ready to try.

"What do you recommend, Germain?"
"The Cognac."

Fat John intervenes. "It's sweet?"

"Not really. But, it works. If you want something sweet, have rum instead."

Germain fills two small glasses - one with Cognac and one with rum.
The sip of alcohol stings the mouth and burns as it goes down but it also lightens the heavy work of digestion. Fat John pours himself another glass of rum and a Cognac for Marcel. This time just to sip.

A few soldiers flirt with the nurses. The officers mainly enjoy their drinks and cigars.

Marcel and Fat John, comfortably seated in the Chesterfields, look at each other. They have had a good evening, but their eyelids are getting heavy.

"Fat John. I think I'll be enjoying my bed soon."

"Me too, Marcel."

They salute the other soldiers who are not in much better shape than them but who remain out of pride. Marcel and Fat John go upstairs and wish each other good night in the hallway.

When he gets in his room, Marcel finds striped pajamas folded on his bed. He closes the curtains and undresses. He puts on his clean, ironed pajamas that smell like lavender. He slips into his bed and falls asleep almost as soon as his head is on the pillow. It is not yet nine o'clock and a deep, dreamless sleep carries him away from all the hells of war.

The next morning, it is past nine o'clock when Marcel wakes up. For a few seconds, he doesn't know where he is. Then, he smiles and gets up. At the small sink in the bedroom, he throws some water on his face to freshen up. He gets dressed and goes downstairs. In the dining room, he finds Fat John who is stuffing his face with large slices of bread and jam.

"Slept well, Fat John?"

With his mouth full, Fat John can't answer, but he gives a thumbs up.

Angèle, in charge of the morning service, asks Marcel.

"Tea, Coffee or Chocolate?"
"Chocolate, please." answers Marcel with a smile.

After the huge breakfast, Marcel and Fat John make plans for the day.
Fat John suggests, "Let's write a letter to Agnès."

"I have a better idea.... Let's write several. I'm in the mood."

With a big grin, Fat John answers, "Okay."

"But first, a good bath!"
"Always okay."

An hour later, Marcel and Fat John are seated at a round table on the back terrace.

The inn provided paper, pencils and postcards. Fat John talks about everything and nothing but especially about Agnès. Marcel writes. For nearly two hours, they will savor all their little pleasures - joking, laughing, sharing, talking about everything... and Marcel writes, writes and writes some more. He has taken a liking to writing sweet words.

At noon, they are called for lunch. Germain joins them at their table.

"I will be leaving to go back to the trenches today with some of the other soldiers. It's your turn to welcome and take care of the next soldiers arriving."

"No problem, Germain." replies Marcel. At the end of the meal, they all shake hands and Marcel wishes Germain good luck.

The soldiers, now back in uniform, leave on foot just like they arrived. Soon others will replace them. And tomorrow, it will be Marcel and Fat John's turn to go back down the road to hell.

Marcel turns to Fat John. "You know what I prefer here? Sleeping. And now, I'm going to take a good nap. Then tonight, I can enjoy the bar a little longer."

In his room, Marcel undresses and finds himself completely naked. He decides to take advantage of the softness of the sheets and slips into his bed without his pajamas. Marcel drifts off into a good three-hour nap.

Around five o'clock in the afternoon, he returns to the living room where Fat John joins him. They toast together and prepare to welcome new soldiers who are clean and smell of soap. Introductions with ranks and units are made. Fat John introduces them to the bar.

After invading the Chesterfields and deciding the war will never end, the soldiers talk about their civilian lives - married, single, with children or not, factory work, etc. Finally, Anna, the nurse, invites them to the dining room for dinner and sits at Marcel's table along with Fat John and others.

Marcel thanks Anna for joining them. It's a nice touch of femininity that all the soldiers appreciate and need. Anna thanks Marcel with a smile.

After soup and beer, a delicious smell fills the room - roasted chicken. There are cries of joy from all the tables. The cries are doubled when the soldiers realize there will be a whole chicken for each of them. They don't have to eat everything. They can choose their favorite pieces. For gourmet stomachs, there is also dessert. Tonight, it is a big bowl of rice pudding with as much sugar as you want. Fat John is delighted.

Back in the living room, Marcel offers the new soldiers a small shot of alcohol to help their digestion.

This evening, Marcel is not tired and intends to take full advantage of all that is offered in this almost luxurious inn. After two hours of heated discussions of misfortune with the other soldiers and many small glasses of Cognac, Marcel decides to retire but not before another bath in the hot water.

After he says goodnight to everyone, he heads for the bathrooms leaving Fat John with his tall glass of Havana rum.

A few minutes later, he savors the hot water in which he bathes. Tonight, he added two little pleasures. First, a cigar. It's the first cigar he's ever had and he smokes it slowly for full enjoyment. Second, a large balloon glass of Cognac which he sips slowly, too. Regularly, he adds hot water to the bathtub and the vapors mix with the smoke of his cigar.

Marcel tells himself that man adapts well to easy life - he quickly gets used to the pleasures he has at the inn. It would be heaven if he didn't have to go back to hell. Without excessive philosophy, Marcel gets out of the bathtub, dries off and gets dressed. He goes up to his room and tells himself that he's going to enjoy a good night's sleep in a big bed with clean sheets. And, he decides he will not sleep in pajamas like he did for the nap.

Just as he climbed in between the sheets of the bed, there is a small knock on his door and it opens. It's Anna, the nurse. "I have to come to take your temperature."

Marcel, a little embarrassed, asks, "Now?"

"Yes."

She walks over and sits on the edge of the bed. Marcel thinks that the opportunity is too good and tries his luck. He puts his hand on Anna's thigh...

Anna won't leave his room until an hour later and will leave Marcel asleep with a smile on his face.

The next morning, Marcel wonders if he was dreaming. He goes down to the bathroom and prepares his last hot bath before leaving. A few minutes later, he is joined by Fat John.

Marcel doesn't know if he should say anything about his nocturnal adventure, but Fat John is already starting to talk.

"Last night, a nurse came into my room. She wanted to take my temperature. I sent her away....nicely but firmly. I told her to come back in the morning. But this morning, I didn't see anyone!"

After a few seconds of reflection, Marcel bursts out laughing. He realizes it's all part of the leave package.

Fat John is surprised. "What's so funny?"

Marcel laughs twice as hard. He is relieved. He knows now there will be no expectations of courting or marriage from Anna.

"Come on, Fat John. We're going to eat. It's what we do best. I'll explain later."

Fat John, still not sure of why Marcel is laughing, follows his friend to the dining room. At the table, Marcel approaches one of the new soldiers on leave and gives him Germain's instructions for welcoming new soldiers. Then, he turns to Fat John. "We're going to take two large cups of hot chocolate and go to the terrace to write a letter to Agnès."

Seated at the back of the inn, Fat John begins to talk while Marcel takes his notebook to write down his latest adventures. He raises his head and says to Fat John. "Don't you think there are too many nurses and not enough injured people?"

"There are no injured at all!"
"Conclusion?"
"What conclusion? I don't know!"
"Ha! I guess today I'm going to write about your faithfulness!"
"Well, okay. Yeah...if you want to."

Thus passes the morning, with the laughing gaze of Marcel and the innocent eyes of Fat John.

Breaking the silence and daydreams, Marcel attracts the attention of Fat John. "Don't you think this is even better than Christmas?"

Fat John smiled at him. "Yes, it's Christmas in July!"

After lunch, Marcel and Fat John return to their rooms to prepare for their journey back to the trenches.

Sitting on his bed, Marcel looks around the room. He wants to print in his mind all the details of where he slept two nights, took a nap and enjoyed a one-night stand. He puts on his clean new uniform and goes down to the living room. There, he finds Fat John, Lieutenant Beauséjour and a sergeant he does not know. The introductions are made and the lieutenant advises. "The sergeant is going back to the same trench as you. You'll escort him, won't you, Soldier Marcel?"

"Of course, lieutenant." replies Marcel.

The lieutenant wishes them safe travels, good luck and hopes to see them again soon.

*

Françoise asks Louise, "How do you know all this? Did Marcel let you read his notebook?"

"Marcel had a lot of notebooks. Over time, he gave them all to me to read. Except the one when he was on leave. I had to insist. He had never shown that one to our dear sister, Jeanne."

"I imagine not!"
"You know how men are... They like to brag a bit."
"Obviously!"

"So, I didn't push it. Then one evening, he pulled out the notebook he kept during his leave while Jeanne was in the kitchen cooking dinner. That's how I know all that."

"You're a little sneaky, aren't you."

Louise, suddenly pensive, says, "Afterwards, it was horrible...those poor, poor soldiers."

*

The three soldiers left on their way back to the devil's den of trenches. The silence was almost deafening as they dreaded their return. As they got closer, they hear the sound of cannons. Weakly at first, then louder and louder. They meet other soldiers along the way. Some are couriers, others are on leave, the last are stretcher-bearers carrying the wounded to the infirmary station.

When they arrive in their trench, Marcel and Fat John look around to find familiar faces. Finally, they reunite with Fons and Isidore.

Fons is all smiles and Isidore groans. "It was terrible here. We took it in the mouth while you were gone, guys."

Marcel replies, "I know it. I was the one that ordered the shells."

The four friends look at each other and burst out laughing.

Fons wants to know. "So how was the leave?"

"It's really good, guys," replies Marcel.
"Ah yes, it's really good," confirms Fat John.
"Come on, guys. Tell us more," insists Isidore.

Marcel gives some details.

"It's a two-hour walk from here. Very nice house. Well kept. We slept in nice rooms, in good beds with nice sheets. We ate like at home. There is a bathroom with large bathtubs. And cold beer is unlimited. What else, Fat John?

"You forgot the rum!"
"And the Cognac!"
"And the nurses!"
"Ah yes, the nurses! If you have a temperature!

Marcel will not say more. The morale of the soldiers has already improved. They must not only protect their line of defense but also their inn - the haven of all those small daily pleasures which they have been deprived of for so long.

Fons and Isidore look at each other. "This leave sounds very good."

Marcel teases with a raised finger. "Yes, but you will have to be good boys, do all your duties and be vigilant every day before you can go."

Fons bounces in immediately. "Speaking of vigilance, I feel like the frequency of artillery fire has calmed down a bit. But that's just my impression. Does anyone have any idea when it's going to stop?"

"No. No one," replies Marcel.

Meanwhile the canteen is available and the soldiers go to the third trench with their bowls. Marcel and Fat John look at each other. They shrug their shoulders. Back to normal and the daily life of the soldier.

In the evening, the soldiers fall asleep in their "coffin" holes, ready to jump at the slightest alarm.

At 4:30 a.m., most of the soldiers are already alert and ready for the day. The sun is not up yet and Fons must go on a courier mission.

When he returns later that day, Fons has a strange look on his face. He calls his friends away from the others to tell them the secrets he's learned.

"I have good news and very bad news. The good news is that everyone is running out of shells. So, fighting will be less fierce. The very bad news is the Germans will soon be using gases."

The news of gases hits Marcel, Fat John and Isidore like a slap in the face. This is indeed very bad news. They don't have gas masks.

"What are we going to do, Marcel?"
"I don't know. We'll ask our sergeant."

Sergeant Bonmariage is a little further in the trench. They wait for him to approach and Marcel speaks to him.

"Sergeant, there's a rumor saying that the Germans are going to use gas. But, we don't have gas masks."

"Soldier, for now, the Germans will not use gas. The wind is coming from the south. If they throw gas, it will blow back to them."

"The wind could change direction."

"Yes, of course. I'll go to see if I can find out any more information and come back to you."

Marcel is distraught. His friends watch him. Finally, he says, "He's going to find out. But, he didn't deny it. So Fons' information must be true."

Everyone is waiting for the sergeant to return.

After the constant fear from the bombardments, it will not be the shells and firing that is the mortal enemy. It will be the gases that arrive without sound and slip into the trenches to take you while you sleep.

Two hours later, the sergeant is back. He has his arms full of small terrycloth towels and gathers his soldiers around him.

"Here, soldiers. The news is not good. The Germans are going to throw gas at us and we have no masks. The factories in the rear are working hard and we will soon be equipped. For the moment, German gases are not lethal. They sting the eyes and the throat. We have one solution until the masks are available."

The sergeant takes a small towel, no bigger than a handkerchief, and explains. "At the first gas alarm, you take out your towels and you pee on them. You hide in your holes with the towel on your face. This will neutralize the gases."

No soldier reacts. They are trying to imagine themselves peeing on their towels.

The sergeant is ready to leave, but turns back to his men.

"I almost forgot. Our factories are also manufacturing gas. So, be brave, soldiers. We're gonna WIN this war!"

Over the next few days, the shelling comes at a slower, but nonetheless, continuous pace and the soldiers continued to dive into their "coffin" holes. The forward guard post of the Bonmariage platoon still stands. It receives hits but it has resisted destruction. Every day the soldiers repair it.

The wind continues to blow from the south.

One of the soldiers made a primitive weather vane to track the direction of the wind. This reassures everyone…..a little. Everyone obsesses over the direction of the wind. From time to time, a German shot makes the weather vane spin like a top. The enemy finds this funny. The soldiers of Sergeant Bonmariage do not laugh.

At the end of the summer, the wind suddenly changed direction and the first gases were launched and crawled into the allied trenches. Marcel, like the others, peed on his towel and covered his face. In the eerie silence of waiting for the gases to evaporate, he heard Isidore's voice. He was not praying. He was talking to himself -- "Surely, I'll go to heaven, because I am in hell here."

Later, Marcel will write Isidore's words in his notebook.

Ten, twenty, maybe more times, they put that pee-soaked towel on their face in disgust. But eventually, there is no more disgust - just shame and anger. The soldiers cannot wait to launch their gas as soon as the wind turns.

In November, all the allied forces received military supplies which were quickly distributed. Along with the new rifles and cartridge belts, the soldiers received gas masks.

Military engineering companies send platoons into the trenches to install rainwater harvesting systems and purifying tanks to make the rain suitable for drinking and other uses. Away from the trenches, they set up latrines made of canvas tents and wooden planks. They bring tons of hay for the soldiers to sleep on. Hay is also wedged into all the holes in the trenches in an attempt to dry up stagnant pools of water. At least it makes the trenches dry. They are no longer a cesspool of mud and rats. They're a dry cesspool with rats. The number of braziers has been doubled.

Pots and ovens are installed on metal carts to create mobile kitchens and "soup men" come with meals three times a day.

All the supplies are French manufactured. Belgian soldiers cannot call upon the industrial, agricultural or human resources of their country because it is occupied and controlled by a foreign army. The King's soldiers must rely on the generosity of their allies, and fortunately, they do not let them down.

The English canine brigades also assist by bringing dogs for hunting rats in the trenches. The rats almost outnumber the soldiers, and despite the bounties given to soldiers for each dead rat, the rats thrive with ease in the dirty and muddy trenches.

A dog was given to each company and two soldiers were allocated to each dog.

Sergeant Bonmariage joins the trench of his men. "Soldiers... you see we're taking care of you. It's not a luxury, but things are improving. And it's not over. We will organize a rotation of troops between the first, second and third lines. "You will not stay more than five days on the front line. After that, you will go to the third line for a little rest and you can wash in hot water. But you will have to remain vigilant. In the event of an alert, we will all defend the line. Got it, soldiers? Go to your posts! We're gonna WIN this war!"

The soldiers are happy to get a little more comfort, a little less rats, regular meals and a little rest.

Marcel, Fat John, Isidore and Fons are sitting in their holes on the front line. Everyone seems happy with the improvements made to their daily lives. Everyone except Marcel.

Fons asks him. "Why are you sulking, Marcel?"

Marcel looks at his three friends who are caught in the terrible throws of war with him. "Are you happy?"

Isidore replies, "It's better than nothing. It's getting a little better. We won't have to wait until next Christmas to be able to wash up. "

Fons continues, "What's on your mind, Marcel?"

Marcel replies, "So, you don't understand what's going on? All these improvements? It's because we're here forever. If we don't die from a bullet, a shell or gas, we're going to die of old age. The officers know very well that the war will last for years.

The group's mood plummeted.

"Do you really believe what you're saying, Marcel?" asks Fat John.

"Of course. Nothing has moved for months. Do you think the Germans are going to apologize and go home?"

Marcel's three friends look at each other. They don't know what to say.

Marcel continues.

"I'll show you how much I believe it. I bet five cents we'll spend Christmas here and all of next year. Who wants to bet with me?"

As if to ward off fate, everyone pulls out five cents to bet against Marcel. They will lose all their bets. It will be another Christmas in the trenches.

This Christmas of 1915 will not be at all like the one of 1914. The violence of the conflict has taken on proportions never imagined. The dead and wounded have been too numerous and the relentlessness of military victory is too celebrated.

At midnight, December 24, the firing stopped long enough for a few fir trees and a few white flags to be erected. There is some faint humming of a Christmas carol that travels from man to man and trench to trench.
"*Silent Night*" will be without words, but will remain full of hope - the hope of having a silent night. But, even that hope dwindles.

*

"Do you remember what we did at Christmas 1915?" Louise asks.

"I have to think about it..." replies Françoise.
"Well, you were already sixteen. You should remember."
"Ah yes, I remember... I was stealing sips of brandy from mother's glass."
"You didn't."
"Yes, I did. And an hour later, I fell asleep. It made me drunk."

They both burst out laughing.

*

The truce only lasts 24 hours. Nobody knows who started planting the white flags and nobody knows who started taking them down. Regardless, it's over.

Marcel goes to see Fat John, Isidore and Fons to collect the money from his bet. Everyone complains a little, except Marcel.

"Hand over your nickels, guys."

Isidore tries a question. "Wasn't the bet for the whole year?"

"No. That's another bet! Who wants to take a chance? You can't win if you don't take a chance! Come on, guys, lighten up. Okay, we're in hell. But, we can try to have a little fun."

Marcel's friends put their hands in their pockets to bet hoping they will be right this time.

The year 1916 begins with a harsh and dry cold but the spring will be early. It has been nearly two years since the conflict began and all around the trenches the landscapes are dead. All the trees have been destroyed. There is no longer a blade of grass. The gases killed all the vegetation. All that remains is the brown, dirty earth. Dry in summer and muddy the rest of the time. All other colors are gone. The "no man's land" is strewn with shell holes and barbed wire. The few surrounding farms are no more than ruins. The trace of people have disappeared. There are only soldiers and weapons left.

So many soldiers have been killed. Nobody knows the numbers, but there are a lot of them. The seriously wounded do not return to the battlefields and the number of men left in the countries to come and fight are beginning to run out. The new soldiers are either too young or too old. Fons had heard that the new soldiers coming to reinforce the lines are prisoners taken from jails.

The newcomers receive their initiation to the horror of the war from the first day and every day after.

Because every day, whether by God or the Devil, the infernal din of shells and bullets rips the silence without warning. You have to run in the holes and try to shield your ears, but it's useless. The violence of noise enters the gut and destroys from within.

And every day, whether by God or the Devil, dead and wounded are evacuated. This deadly game of cat and mouse wears down the patience, humor and strength of the soldiers. The remaining soldiers become undead. All motivation for fighting is gone. Only survival matters.

And every day, whether by God or the Devil, the end of the war gets further and further away. Sleepless nights swallow up the days and despair swallows up hope of better days.

And as if that were not enough, a new weapon makes its appearance.

In the spring, for the first time, the German planes equipped with machine guns fly over the trenches in northern France. There are two soldiers in the plane – a pilot and a gunner. The gunner fires bullets and also takes pictures to report back to the officers.

Marcel, like all the others, is hidden in his "coffin" hole.

"Isidore, can you adjust your machine gun to shoot skyward?"
"Yes, probably."
"It would be nice if you could shoot down that plane circling us."
"That's a good idea."
"You might even get a medal."
"I'll work on that right away."
"Good."

For several days, Isidore tinkered with his machine gun so that he could easily detach it from its support and point it towards the sky.

Isidore made sure he asked Sergeant Bonmariage for permission. Authorization granted.

Isidore approaches Marcel. "Tomorrow, I'm going to try to shoot a plane."
Marcel smiles and pats Isidore on the shoulder. "I'm curious to see that."

The next day, Sergeant Bonmariage arrives in the front line trench and approaches Marcel. "Soldier Marcel. It's your turn."

"My turn?"
"Your turn at the inn. Are you going back with Fat John?"
"Fat John? Yes, of course."

Marcel is already daydreaming about his next few days. Everything flashes back to him - the long hot baths, the roasted chicken, the beef stews, the Cognac, the Chesterfield armchairs, the long sleeps in clean sheets, his first cigar and, of course, Anna. He had almost forgotten about her...but not really.

The sergeant pulls him out of his daydreams.

"Here are your leave papers. Gather your things. Get Fat John and get the hell out of here."

"Yes, Sergeant."
"... And have a good time."
"Thank you, Sergeant."

Marcel leans into his hole and picks up a few things. In his head, he organizes his leave. He can already see it. He wonders if Anna will be there, if there will be chicken, if he will have the same room ... and if maybe there will be something new. Marcel likes surprises.

He gets up and goes to find Fat John.

The thoughts of his next few days occupy his mind. He intends to take full advantage of it to recharge all his energies and to smoke his second cigar.

He finds Fat John and calls him to order like a sergeant.

"Soldier Fat John, get up!"

Fat John, with a mocking air, looks at Marcel.

"What's going on, little Marcel?"
"I order you to come with me on leave to the inn."

Fat John jumps out of his hole.
"At your orders, General Marcel."

"Get you things and follow me."

While Fat John is getting ready, he asks Marcel.

"We don't have a sergeant with us?"
"No, it's only on the way back. To prevent us from deserting."
"Ah, good. Are you sure?"
"Yes, have you seen this sergeant that returned with us last time ever again ?"
"Nope."
"Well, I'm sure we'll find him at the inn."
"Good." Fat John doesn't care.

Fat John is already beginning to sing an impromptu tune he created out of his joy.
"I'm going to the inn. You're going to the inn. We're going to the inn."

Marcel and Fat John walk through the maze of trenches away from the front line. Marcel stops and turns to Fat John. "And don't forget to call a nurse if you have a temperature!"

Fat John, unbelievably, still does not understand this joke.

It was then that the shell fell ten yards from them. Shards went in all directions. Marcel, in the front row, was hit directly all over the body and on the face. His body shielded Fat John who was behind him. Fat John was also hit but not as badly.

Marcel drops to the ground.

Without concern of his own injuries, Fat John yells, "Stretcher bearers! Hurry! We have a wounded soldier!"

Fat John leans over to Marcel and rolls him over.

He exclaims in shock. "Oh my God! His face!"

*

"Louise, Marcel couldn't have remembered that."
"No, it was Fat John who told him later."

Françoise remembers the first time she saw Marcel at the ballroom. He was dancing with their older sister, Jeanne.

"When I saw Jeanne's smile, I knew he was the one for her."
"He was taller than her. I know she liked that."
"Poor Marcel. He was so unlucky."
"What? To have met our sister?"

"No, silly. Don't you remember? He was deported to the concentration camps for several years during the Second World War."
"No, I haven't forgotten that."

"When you're unlucky in war, life is miserable."

*

Marcel wakes up. He is lying in a bed. He sees around him a large hospital room with a dozen beds. He turns his head to see the details of the room but it is dark and he cannot see anything. He wonders why the windows are closed and the interior shutters, too.

He wants to get up, but he can't. He wants to talk, but he can't. His ears are working fine. He hears moaning around him. His arms and hands are covered with bandages. His torso, too. And, especially his head. Only his eyes, mouth and nose holes are not covered.

His eyes adapt to the darkness and he sees several beds with wounded. They seem to be in pain. He doesn't feel any pain. He told himself that he must be healed and could probably leave soon. He continues to look around the room and sees nothing in particular. However, he smells this revolting smell of ether which he hates.

He tries to open his mouth without success. He can't move his jaw and no sound comes out of his mouth. Only a low growl is emitted from his throat. With his left hand, he hits the metal post of his bed. He wants to get the attention of a nurse or a doctor.

A nurse arrives, but it's not Anna. Marcel now knows that he is not at the inn. "Hello, Monsieur Marcel. Don't try to talk. You can't."

Marcel sighs.

"I'll bring you a notebook and a pencil."

A few moments later, she returns with a large notebook, three pencils and a doctor who comes to sit on the edge of his bed.

"So, Monsieur Marcel, I'm going to explain what happened to you."

Marcel growls and bangs his left hand on the bed.

The doctor turns to the nurse to take the notebook and pencil and hands them to Marcel who begins to write.

"Where am I?"
"At the War Wounded Hospital in Amiens."

"How long have I been here?"

"Several months."

"I do not remember."
"You're on morphine. We put you to sleep so you wouldn't suffer."

"What day is today?"
"February 7, 1917. It's a Wednesday."

"When can I go out?"
"Oh my! Not so fast, my friend. We've already fixed a lot of things but there's still a lot to do. So far, we've done the easiest and the fastest. Now we're going take care of your face and especially your jaw."

"When?"
"When you've regained some strength. You've lost a lot of weight and a lot of blood. You're going to have to gain weight, generate blood and make bone."

"I'm hungry."
"Very well. Your nurse, Sister Theresa, will take care of you."

Marcel no longer writes. He is waiting for his next meal which will be served to him by Sister Theresa.

After a few minutes, she arrives with a large bowl and sits down on the edge of the bed. She plunges a spoon into the soup and places it on Marcel's lips. He swallows this nectar as if he hadn't eaten for ages. In fact, it's a simple pea soup with small pieces of bacon. He doesn't have to chew. Anyway, he can't.

After what seems like a royal meal to him, Marcel falls asleep for several hours.

When he wakes up, he sees thin rays of sunlight through the gaps in the interior shutters but he doesn't know if it's morning or afternoon. The other patients can't help him. All they do is moan all the time. So he waits lying still in the bed. Besides, he can't move.

He sees Sister Theresa wandering around the room going from patient to patient. When she arrives at his bedside, it's with a bowl of soup. He wishes he could smile at her.

For weeks, this will be his routine and he feels his strength slowly returning. He also feels his appetite for life and his awakening memory.

He remembers the war, his friends, the sergeant, the trenches, the shells, the gas. Everything is slowly coming back. But there aren't many happy memories. There is the first Christmas, the one of 1914. There is Christmas in July at the inn, Christmas of 1915 which was on minimum service. The last Christmas he spent on morphine and does not remember.

Marcel searches his memory for happy memories. It is through the little pleasures of the past that he wants to come back to life. No gloom. He thinks about musette balls, pretty girls on Saturday nights, chocolate, friends …

After several weeks, the doctor is back at Marcel's bedside. He tells him they are scheduling his next operation which will be on his right arm.

Marcel takes his big notebook.

"What operation?"

"The bones of the right forearm have been broken in several places and they have not mended properly. We will try to repair them."

"And my jaw?"
"Later, Marcel."

"What is your name?"
"Gilbert."

"Thank you, Doctor Gilbert."

Fifteen days later, while Sister Theresa is removing the bandages from Marcel's forearm, Doctor Gilbert arrives, examines Marcel and gives his patient some more news.

"Everything went well, Marcel."

"Thanks," writes Marcel on his notebook.

"But there's still one problem. You won't be able to turn your right palm up."

"What?"
"You will not be able to beg."

"I've never begged. I'm not going to start."
"Fine. So, if you don't mind, we'll leave your right arm as it is."

Marcel closes his eyes, shakes his head in approval and goes back to sleep.

Marcel finds the time in the hospital long. The bandages are fewer and fewer. There are less and less heavy doses of morphine. But the time is dragging. Fortunately, he can now eat his soup on his own. Messy, but he can do it himself. He is neither skillful with his hands nor with his lips which are still numb.

When he feels more strength returning to his body Doctor Gilbert suggested another operation.

"Marcel, I really want to install an external metal prosthesis on your jaw for you."

Marcel does not know what to think.

"That'll keep the bones together and we can remove some of the bandages from your head. What do you say, soldier? And, with the prosthesis, you could try talking a little,... chewing a little?"

Marcel is afraid. He writes.

"Forever?"
"No, Marcel. It would be a temporary solution. We're waiting for the X-ray machine from Paris. It will allow us to see what's going on inside. And then we can operate on your jaw for good."

Marcel completes the sheet of his notebook.

"Go for it!"

The doctor smiles at him and pats him on the shoulder.

When Sister Theresa comes to give him his next meal, Marcel writes two words in his big notebook.

"Fat John?"

The nurse reads and tells Marcel, "Write me everything you know about him. Family name, number, army corps, address, anything you know."

Marcel nods and begins writing down everything he knows about Fat John except his address which he does not know. The nurse reads it and looks Marcel in the eye.

"I'll take care of it, but it may take weeks, maybe months."

In the meantime, Marcel decides he is going to write a letter to Fat John. When he's finished, he realizes he doesn't have his address. He rolls his eyes at his stupidity and begins a letter for Sergeant Bonmariage.

"Dear Sergeant,

I am writing to tell you I am in Amiens hospital. I'm not dead - at least not yet. My body has suffered but is on the mend. On the other hand, my jaw is not yet repaired and it could take a few more months.

I hope this letter finds you in good health and that you continue to take good care of your men. If you have time to write to me, I would like to hear news of my friends: Fat John, Fons and Isidore.

I wish you good luck, Sergeant.
A lot of luck !

Soldier Marcel."

He gives his letter to the nurse with a small piece of paper on which he has written all the sergeant's information. And, a big "THANK YOU" at the bottom of the note.

A week later, Marcel receives an additional dose of morphine and goes into the operating room for the whole day. That evening, he is moved to his bed in the ward. He is still unconscious. Sister Theresa puts bandages around his jaw so that he does not hurt himself. They give him another dose of morphine to ensure he gets a good night's sleep.

The next day, Marcel wakes up with the doctor and the nurse around his bed. His eyes beg the question. The doctor puts his hand on Marcel's arm.

"The operation went well, Marcel. Now, we are going to remove some bandages. Go ahead, Sister Theresa."

Gently, the nurse removes the first layers. The doctor supports Marcel's chin to avoid a shock. Everything is done very slowly. All the bandages are removed. Marcel can see a metal frame on the side of his face. The doctor and the nurse still support Marcel's chin.

"Slowly try to move your jaw, Marcel."

Marcel tries. He can open and close his mouth. He does the exercise several times. It's not too painful and he starts again. The doctor and nurse have removed their hands from his chin. Marcel noticed the silence in the room. No one is moaning anymore. The sliding curtains around the bed are closed.

"Sister Theresa, go and get a meat broth with meatballs. Something to chew on!"

Sister Theresa leaves and Doctor Gilbert looks at Marcel smiling.

"Do you want to talk?"

He replies, "Yes."

This simple sound is a little stammered, but that's it.

Then, word after word, Marcel gains confidence. He answers questions from Doctor Gilbert, regains his smile and is happy at being back to the living. It's not perfect, but it's so much better. One word at a time. And, just a few words.

When Marcel can slowly chew the meatballs in his tomato soup, his smile confirms his hopefulness and relief. After what is to him a fabulous meal, he falls asleep - almost happy.

Still on morphine, Marcel comes out of his deep sleep a few hours later. He hears movements and whispers around his bed. The curtains are open. He weakly opens his eyes and discovers a veritable "court of miracles". The monsters of war have gathered around his bed.

One of the monsters starts talking.

"So it's you, Marcel?"
"No, it's not him. He's the handsome Marcel."
"We would like to look like him."

All the words intertwine and become confusing for Marcel. This annoys him and he starts to get angry. Is it a dream? A nightmare? He is still on morphine and all these monsters that surround him start to worry him.

"What do you want?"

The closest to him begins. "Good evening, Marcel. They have done a beautiful job on your operation. You look very good."

This simple sentence full of hissing sounds is barely comprehensible. Marcel looks around him and finally understands. They are his roommates. They are all grotesquely disfigured and have come to see the results of Marcel's operation.

Their faces look like a field plowed by a boar and sewn up with a knitting needle. They lack arms, hands and even ears. Marcel suddenly is short of breath. He could speak, but he doesn't have the words.

"Tell us, Marcel. How do we look? Are we good looking like you?"
"We don't have mirrors."
"We do not know."
"We would like to know."
"Everyone is lying to us."
"And between us, we also lie to each other... so..."

Marcel looks at all the desperate men around his bed. They are not ugly. They have lost their humanity. He did not know them before, but today they are no longer men. What makes a human being is the soul, the look and the face. If the face is no longer there, you focus on the gaze and if the gaze has disappeared, you dive into the soul. But all of this takes time, requires willpower and it demands love.

But Marcel has no patience, so he answers carefully.

"Well, you all look very handsome to me. But, since I don't know how you looked before, it's hard for me to tell if you are better or worse."

The monsters look at each other and start laughing.

Marcel's monsters are slowly moving away from his bed. He hears them as they leave.

"Blessed Marcel!"
"What a liar!"
"Yes, but he's funny."

The morphine overcomes him, and Marcel falls asleep again.

After a few weeks, Marcel can finally walk using a cane. He goes around to visit his monsters and gives a small wave to those who are awake.

Every day, one or two of his monsters pass through Doctor Gilbert's operating room. Sometimes with success, but without really leading to human beauty. Marcel is waiting for the X-ray machine so he can get rid of this damn metal frame.

One day in October 1917, Sister Theresa comes to Marcel's bed.

"I don't have a lot of news, but I have one piece of good news. Your friend, Fat John, is not on the death list. However, I don't know where he is."

"Thank you, Sister Theresa. It's very kind of you to take care of this."

Sister Theresa nods and leaves him to rest.

As good news usually comes in pairs, that afternoon Doctor Gilbert comes to tell Marcel the X-ray machine has arrived.

"Next week, we start the X-rays for everyone!"

All of Marcel's monsters are X-rayed and surgeries follow at a good pace. It is now Marcel's turn.

The doctor is at Marcel's bedside explaining the agenda.

"Operation one: Remove the outer metal frame. Operation two: Bind three pieces of jaw bone together with small metal pieces. Some small bones have already fused together. Are we okay to proceed, Marcel?"

"Okay."

A week later, Marcel is in bed. He's still on morphine. The outer splint is no longer there. It will be necessary to wait until he wakes up to remove the bandages. It will be done tomorrow.

The next morning, Doctor Gilbert examines the chin.

"Does it hurt here, Marcel?"
"A little, but it's tolerable."
"Open your mouth."

The doctor dips two fingers in to make sure there are no open or bleeding wounds.

"Alright! A few more weeks of rehabilitation and everything should be fine."

During rehabilitation, Marcel asks to see the doctor.

"Doctor, I don't think my jaw is set properly."
"Let me see."

The doctor puts his hands under Marcel's jaws and feels for a long time.

"Yes, there is a little wobbling."
"Yes, it floats a bit."
"Does it hurt?"
"Yes, a little, but I can bear it."

"Marcel, you're not naïve. I'm going to explain to you with as much honesty as possible. We cannot do any more operations. The flesh under your jaw is too damaged. It would do more harm than good."

"So I stay like this?"
"It bothers you?"
"Sometimes, it feels like my jaw drops or my mouth is hanging open."

The doctor continues his examination and thinks at the same time.

"How about a chin strap?"
"What is that?"
"A small sling that attaches behind the ears and holds the chin."

Marcel is skeptical.
The doctor calls his assistant.

"Go to the medicine cabinets and bring me some chin straps."

A few minutes later, Marcel is trying out the different chin straps. The doctor turns into a traveling salesman and explains the advantages and disadvantages of each strap.

"So, Marcel, have you made your choice?"
"Not really."
"Okay, Marcel, take one in leather. It's stronger. Take two in fabric. It's lighter."

Marcel picks up the straps on the table not realizing they will become permanent accessories in his life.

It is now December 1917 and Christmas is approaching.

Marcel is called into Doctor Gilbert's office.

"Hello Marcel. How are you? And how's that jaw?"
"It's the same."
"Marcel, I have good news for you. You can leave the hospital. The last exams are good. You can go home!"

"Ah, yes? And how do I do that? My country is occupied by the Germans. Do you think they will let me pass?"

"Shit. I forgot. You're not French. You don't have a place to go?"

"No. I have no family and I haven't heard from my sergeant. I don't know where my friends are."

"You could join your King in Coxyde."

"To do what? You know very well that I have been declared unfit for combat."

"I'm sorry, Marcel. I hadn't thought of all that. Do you know what you want to do?"

"I have an idea, but you have to agree."

"Tell me, Marcel. If I can help you..."

"I would like to stay here and help my little monsters. They call me the handsome Marcel. They are in much worse shape than me. Besides, it will relieve Sister Theresa. I will be able to help her with all sorts of tasks."

The doctor is surprised. It is the first time a patient wants to stay in the hospital. "It's very generous of you, Marcel. But there is a problem. I might need your bed for a new injured person."

"You do have a little cubby hole where I could sleep, don't you?"
"You really want to stay, huh!"

Marcel nods and smiles.

The doctor continues.

"Is your smile because you're happy or is it part of rehabilitation?"
"Both, sir."
"Come on! I'm going to call Sister Theresa and introduce her to her new assistant. I'm sure she'll be delighted."

*

"Is that why Marcel was so familiar with caretaking and medicine?" Françoise asks Louise.

"Yes. Every cloud has a silver lining. Anyway, it served us well. Well, especially me. Without him, I think I would be dead. Don't you remember?"

"No, I wasn't there. I had a new fiancé."

"Well, Marcel was there for me. He walked halfway across town to a pharmacy. It was a Sunday night and he got back just in time...before I choked."

"What was wrong with you?"

"A bag of blood on my throat. It had suddenly swelled up and I was having more and more trouble breathing."

"And Marcel, what did he do?"

"He brought back a dozen leeches and placed them on the blood bag. These dirty beasts feasted. Regularly, Marcel removed a leech and plunged it into salt water to make it throw up the blood. Then, he put it back to the blood bag. After twenty minutes, I could breathe normally again. After two hours, it was over. He made me drink a thick sticky liquid. Voila! I was cured."

"Thank you, Marcel." concludes Louise.

*

Marcel takes his new mission very seriously. All day long, he helps Sister Theresa. Marcel's monsters are happy that their comrade has stayed with them.

The end of the year is approaching and Marcel, with Sister Theresa's smile and Doctor Gilbert's approval, wants to organize something special for Christmas Eve.

For the first time in a year, Marcel leaves the hospital and goes to the forest. He looks for a bush or a small shrub to act as a fir tree - just like the ones at the trenches in 1914. He sets his sights on a small shrub full of red berries.

He places his shrub on the large table in the center of the room and puts small candles around it. This evening, the meal is special – roasted chicken. Marcel goes around the beds to help those who cannot eat alone.

It still smells of morphine and ether, but there's a hint of Christmas and everyone tries to smile. They make peace with their wounds. A few Christmas carols will be sung during the evening. A little wine will be served.

Doctor Gilbert enters the room, sits down at the large table and pours himself a glass of wine. "Gentlemen, my sister, I wish you a Merry Christmas!"

All those who can, raise their glasses to the doctor's health and wish a Merry Christmas.

"The news of the conflict is not too bad. You know the first American troops arrived on our soil in the spring of this year. They call them "Sammies" – the sons of Uncle Sam. After having installed all the logistics, barracks, ports and military airports, plus the railways, American soldiers were trained in French arms and our largest armament factories delivered everything they needed - guns, shells, rifles, bullets and tanks.

"At the beginning of November, the Americans left to attack the Germans. I would be surprised if we celebrate Christmas next year without a conclusion to this war."

He raises his glass again, clears his throat and continues.

"Anyway, the Americans seem to love Christmas. I've had calls from half a dozen fellow surgeons who work with the American contingents. All their barracks are decorated, they sing Christmas songs non-stop and, since this morning, huge turkeys have been cooking in the ovens. The turkeys are really huge it seems. They must have brought them on the boats because here the turkeys aren't that big."

Everyone laughs and Doctor Gilbert leaves the room, saluting with his glass and punctuating the gesture with a final "Merry Christmas."

Sitting on his bed, Marcel realizes that none of his monsters have visitors this Christmas

Eve. In fact, he never saw any visitors in the room. Maybe the monsters just don't want to be seen. Ah yes, he remembers. A few months ago a woman had entered the room. Sister Theresa had shown her the bed where her husband was sleeping. As she approached, she gave a gasp of horror and ran out crying. We never saw her again.

From the spring of 1918, the American offensives multiplied and the Germans lost more and more battles. The armies of the Kaiser begin to lose ground.

It was in May 1918 that Marcel began to organize walks on the hospital grounds. At the end of the afternoon, when all the other patients are waiting or eating their meals, Marcel takes his little monsters out to get some fresh air. It can only do them good. With the help of stretchers and wheelchairs, everyone finds themselves in the park.

"Thank you, beautiful Marcel"

This is what Marcel heard the most after the first walk. Marcel is happy. He feels like he's done good. He will continue the walks every day throughout the summer.

Meanwhile, the fighting is raging. The new French guns, more powerful and more precise, are doing damage to the German lines. The Renault assault tanks are destroying the German trenches one by one. And at the controls of all these new weapons are fresh and well-trained troops - the American soldiers.

Every day before the "Monster Walk", Marcel passes by Doctor Gilbert's office to steal the newspaper. He sits on the park bench to read it while keeping an eye on his new friends. When he has finished reading the newspaper, he writes a few words in his notebook.

One day, the doctor didn't give Marcel time to steal his newspaper. The doctor bursts into the monster room yelling, "The war is over!"

As of today, November 11, 1918 at 11:00am, the war is finally over.

Cries of joy are heard throughout the hospital. The news spreads from room to room like wildfire. Anyone who can move runs into the halls to make sure it's true. When they see the headline on the front page of the newspaper, a huge smile finally appears on their faces - a smile of relief.

The next day, Marcel asks the doctor, "Doctor Gilbert, do you think I can go back to my country?"

"You've always been free to leave, Marcel. But give me a couple of days to find out. I'll call the Coxyde military hospital. If they give me the green light, you can go."

"Thank you, Doctor."

"Marcel, one last thing. Do not sneak out like a thief in the night. Say goodbye to your little monsters."

"Of course."

Two days later, before any news from Coxyde arrives, Marcel receives a completely unexpected visit. A soldier comes to tell him a visitor is waiting for him in the park. Surprised, Marcel goes to the park and immediately recognizes a familiar face. Seated on his favorite bench is Sergeant Bonmariage.

They shake hands vigorously and pat each other on the shoulder.

"Sergeant Bonmariage!"
"Soldier Marcel."
"Not for long. I'm going to Coxyde soon to be discharged. But you, sergeant, how are you?"
"As you see, I'm still in one piece!"

The sergeant looks carefully at Marcel's face. He can clearly see that the left side and the right side are not quite the same, but it doesn't seem too dramatic to him.

"I was afraid for you, Marcel. But I see that it's not too serious."

"No, it's fine. You should see my roommates. My God, poor people, they're beat up and physically destroyed."

They sit on the bench and continue their conversation.

"Sergeant, have you heard from my friends?"
"Didn't you get my letter?"
"No,"
"Ah! I thought you already knew."
"Knew what?"

"So, Isidore was killed. He was in the open with his machine gun and an airplane shot at him. He was hit in the head several times. His skull exploded. It was a horrible sight."

"Fons got to where he could not withstand the constant bombardments and he lost his nerves. He was crying all the time. We spoke to him, he did not answer. We sent him to the infirmary. I don't know where he is now."

"And Fat John?"

"Fat John was with you when you took the shards but you took the major hit and your body protected him. He was barely hit and not in the face. We sent him to the infirmary also. Last I heard, they had transferred him to Coxyde. He was unfit for combat. That's all I know."

The sergeant continues to give more details of the course of the war during the last months.

"In winter '17, we saw the Senegalese arrive in our trenches. The soldiers did not know what to think. Most of them had never seen a black person in their lives. The Senegalese were shocked. They had never been so cold. Everyone adapted quickly."

"Where did these Senegalese come from?"

"Military contingents from the French colonies. Great soldiers! They knew how to shoot, fight, and everything. And, brave at that!"

"Why did they bring them here?"

"There was no one left to replace the dead and wounded. Especially after the carnage of the suicide missions."

"Suicide missions?"

"Yes, they sent soldiers in the "no man's land" to take the German trenches and there was almost no artillery support. For the Germans, it was like pigeon shooting. It stopped when Clemenceau became President of France."

"What madness this war! I thought it was only going to last a few weeks. Four years!"

"There may be some who are happy. Like the carpenters. They have never built so many coffins. We would have to count the coffins to know the number of dead."

"And the wounded, Sergeant!"

"Of course. After that, the politicians and the officers are surprised that soldiers go into mutiny, that soldiers mutilate themselves, that soldiers commit suicide, ... That's hell."

Sergeant Bonmariage catches his breath.

"More than half of my soldiers in the platoon are dead or injured for the rest of their lives. Thankfully, they stopped the deadly gases. Too risky. At the slightest bad gust of wind, you'd take the gas back in your face."

Marcel lets the sergeant speak. Obviously, he needs to get it off his chest.

"The surrounding brick farms and barns were all destroyed. There were even some hamlets that were completely razed. No one could win this war. I can tell you we were happy when we saw the "Sammie's" coming."

The conversation continues, but Marcel is already distracted. The murderous details are really the last things he wants to hear. He has the information he wanted. Now, for sure, he must go to Coxyde to find his friend, Fat John.

The sergeant and Marcel leave each other promising to meet again. At the last moment, he holds the sergeant's arm.

"Thank you, Sergeant Bonmariage . Thank you for all you have done."
"What?"
"For looking after us the way you did."
"It was my duty as a soldier and a sergeant, Marcel."
"Thanks, anyway."

"And we WON this war!"
"Yes, but at what price?"

They shake hands one last time.

The next morning, Marcel prepares his luggage. He stops at each bed, gives a little word of encouragement and hope to each one, and leaves. He takes the train to Coxyde and three hours later he is at his destination. At the station, he asks for the direction of the military hospital and goes for a walk on the seafront.

At the hospital, he gives his military papers to be discharged. It takes a while and he waits. When everything is settled, he asks if he can see Fat John. He is told that he has already gone home. He just missed him.

From the officer, he receives a pile of papers with all kinds of information - the help he can get and the shelters where he can sleep. There are several shelters near the hospital and he decides to stay two or three days... anyway, no one is waiting for him.

He spends his days walking on the sea wall, watching the sea and the waves that come to die in the sand or crash on the breakwaters. He drinks in the first moments of peace. It has been four years since that simple word "peace" seemed real.

At noon, he has lunch at the restaurant and feasts on all the local specialties of his country. On the third day, he takes the train to Brussels. His plan is simple. He will go to a shelter for veterans and war wounded, and tomorrow he will go to the small chocolate factory where he worked before the war.

In the shelter, there is a lot of drinking and a lot of fights – yelling, beatings, bodies falling and bottles breaking. Marcel tries to sleep.

The next day, in front of the Atelier St. Amand he sees the large sign still in place - "*Manufacturing & Craftsmanship of Chocolate*". He enters and recognizes a few faces. Several workers stop working and come to welcome Marcel warmly. They congratulate him without moderation. Attracted by the noise the boss, Leon, comes to see what is happening and sees Marcel. He holds out his arms to him. "Welcome home, Marcel."

Marcel smiles. "It seems that I still have my place here!"
"But, of course, Marcel. Come to my office."

Seated in the boss's office, Leon opens two bottles of beer and they clink glasses.

"So, are you coming back to us?"
"Of course, Monsieur Leon."
"You know Isidore is dead."
"Yes, my sergeant told me. He also told me that Fons had a nervous breakdown."
"That's right. He's here."
"He works here?"
"Yes, I took pity on him. He sweeps the workshop."

Marcel turns around looks through the window and sees Fons sweeping the shop.

"I'm going to say hello to him."
"Marcel, you're going to be disappointed. He doesn't recognize anyone."

Marcel has lost his smile, but leaves the office and goes to Fons.

"Hello, Fons."

Fons looks at him and says, "Hello."

"Don't you know me? It's me, Marcel."
"Hello, Marcel."

There is no light in Fons' eyes. There is something dead in the look. Everything is off. Something went away, not to return. He looks without seeing. He listens without understanding. He raises and lowers his eyebrows too quickly and too often then closes his eyes for a few seconds and starts sweeping again.

Marcel is livid and goes back to Leon's office. He preferred when Fons bothered him.

"I warned you, Marcel."
"How long has he been like this?"
"Since he came back here. It's been a year."

Marcel lets out a long sigh.

Leon holds out his hand to Marcel and gives him an envelope.

Marcel reads, "*For Marcel. From Fat John.*"

"Fat John came here?"
"Yeah. I didn't write the letter."

He opens the envelope and reads.

"*Hello Marcel,*

I hope this letter finds you in good health. I'll give you my address: Patisserie Fat John, place du petit Sablon. You come when you want.

See you soon, I hope.

Fat John."

Not very talkative, Fat John, Marcel thinks. But, it's better than nothing, and now he has his address.

"He still works here?"

"No. His parents died of the Spanish flu and he took over the pastry shop. He does a good job. His cakes are delicious. If he offers you some, don't say no."

"Monsieur Leon, I'll go. I'll be back tomorrow morning."
"Marcel, do me a favor. Go to this address."

Leon handed him a business card which reads: "Clothes for Men."

"It would be nice if you gave up your military uniform. It brings back too many bad memories to people. All the wounds are still open."

"Thank you, Monsieur Leon, but I don't have much money."

"You ask for Monsieur Arthur. He's a friend. He takes care of young soldiers. His son died at the front. It's his way of doing good."

As he's speaking, Monsieur Leon has put some money in an envelope and gives it to Marcel.

"But … "
"No talking."
"Thank you, Monsieur Leon."
"Where are you going to sleep tonight?"
"At the army shelter."

"Ask Monsieur Arthur if he still has a free room above the store. It's not great luxury, but in my opinion, it's better than the shelters."

"I don't know how to thank you, Monsieur Leon."
"Come back tomorrow."

They shake hands and Marcel leaves not before turning to the window and waving to Fons. Fons raises his hand with a small wave in return.

That afternoon, Monsieur Arthur welcomes Marcel to his store. He hugs Marcel as if he was his son.

"So, my boy, are we coming back from the war? A real nightmare, huh! Come on, come on! We'll get you dressed."

An hour later, after taking Marcel's measurements, piles of clothes are lined up on the dressmaking table. There is everything you need - pajamas, jackets, pants, shirts, underwear, socks, shoes and even two caps.

"But, Monsieur Arthur, I don't know when I will be able to pay you for all of this."

"Don't worry, boy. We have time."
"And how am I going to carry all these beautiful clothes?"
"I'll ask my tailor to help us. We'll bring all this up to your room."
"My room?"
"Leon told me you needed…"
"Yes, yes. But it's too much, Monsieur Arthur."
"Not at all. If we don't help each other, who will, huh?"

Ten minutes later, Marcel is in his room on the second floor. He opens the window and looks at the interior gardens. There are no flowers. It's December and the beginning of winter.

After washing at the small sink in the bedroom, Marcel puts on new clothes. Return to civilian life. He leaves with a hurried step to go to Fat John's pastry shop. The day has flown by, and he wants to get there before the shop closes.

He arrives in time and sees Fat John behind the counter picking up the unsold items of the day. Marcel pushes the door open and enters.

"Captain Fat John. Attention!"

Fat John jumps, and seeing Marcel bursts out laughing. He limps from his counter and embraces Marcel in his arms.

"Oh, my Marcel, how glad I am to see you."
"And me, also!"

The reunion is full of vitality, friendship and laughter.

Fat John locks the door, turns off the lights and takes Marcel to the back of the shop.

"Sit down, Marcel. We're going to have a drink. Do you want some rum or a beer?"
"Rum?"
"Well, yes. I make rum cakes. So, I have rum."

Marcel laughs. "I thought you had taken a liking to it at the inn."

"No. No. It's for baking. I only drink a little once in a while."

There will be a lot of laughter that evening in the back of Fat John's pastry shop. But, one also has to eat well, and Fat John and Marcel decide to go out to dinner. The most popular restaurant in the capital is "Chez Leon". The menu does not have many choices. There are only casseroles of mussels but they are so good. Plus, the plates are large and the fries are as many as you want. They're going to have a good time. They know it.

There is silence while they indulge in their meal, but afterwards, Marcel has a question.

"Fat John... what about Agnès?"
"Agnès? You just missed her... She went home."
"To her place?"
"Yes. Still at her parents. They don't want us to live together. We're not married."
"Despite the beautiful letters we wrote?"
"They never arrived."
"Shit!"
"Yes! But don't worry, I'm inviting you over Tuesday evening next week to meet her. For dinner! Okay?"

"Okay, Fat John. What time?"
"Around 7 o'clock in the evening."

After this huge meal, Marcel and Fat John walk together through the streets of the city.

Marcel breaks the silence.

"Tell me, Fat Jean, does it hurt when you walk?"
"Not too much. No. And you, Marcel, does it hurt when you eat?"
"Not too much either."

The next day, Marcel is working in Monsieur Leon's workshop. From time to time, he glances at Fons. What he sees saddens him. Fons sweeps constantly around his feet. Sometimes he talks to himself. And, he moves his eyebrows all the time. Fortunately, the other workers leave him alone.

At eight o'clock on Saturday, Monsieur Leon claps his hands and tells all the workers it is time to leave. Everyone gets ready and starts to go. Fons, too. Marcel watches him leave and follows him with his gaze. Outside, he sees a young girl taking Fons' arm. Marcel is surprised. Monsieur Leon is behind him.

"She's his younger sister. A good soul. She takes care of him."
"Good for him. Poor Fons. He must be lonely."

The next day, despite the cold Marcel goes for a walk in his town. He moves from park to park. He admires his beautiful thousand-year-old city and all its old buildings. He is relieved. He escaped the war without too much damage compared to his friends. He is not dead. He didn't go crazy. He looks a little banged up, but he walks straight.

On Monday, back at the workshop Marcel works on the maintenance of the machines. Nothing too exciting, but he takes pride in his work. Fons is always there without really being there. At the end of the day, Fons leaves with his sister and Marcel goes back to his room.

The next day, Marcel is smiling as he arrives at the workshop. He has nice plans for this evening. He is going to dine at Fat John's and he will meet Agnès. This makes him happy.

He just hopes the future wife of Fat John is a nice girl – not impudent or cunning. But he quickly chases this bad thought from his mind. Knowing Fat John and his joviality, he will have chosen a nice girl. Marcel bought a box of chocolates and a small bouquet of flowers to bring to the dinner. He wants to make a good impression. The first impression is always important because it is often the right one.

At five o'clock in the evening, Monsieur Leon dismisses everyone. The workers respond in unison, "Thank you, boss."

Monsieur Leon continues "... and Merry Christmas!"

"Merry Christmas!" they respond...everyone except Marcel who remains speechless. He forgot!

Monsieur Leon approaches Marcel.

"So, Marcel, aren't you happy?"
"Yes, yes. But I forgot it was Christmas and tonight I'm going to eat at Fat John's."
"Ah yes! That's a problem. You better go now before all the shops close."

He leaves immediately. He is looking for a gift idea, something to say, to do, to buy. When he arrives home, he is getting ready for the Christmas Eve dinner and suddenly he has an idea!

Promptly at seven o'clock, he knocks on the door of the pastry shop and Fat John opens it to greet him.

"Come in, Marcel, I'm going to introduce you to Agnès."

Marcel gives the chocolates to Fat John who is already feasting his eyes on the box.

In the back room, Fat John nudges Marcel.

"Marcel, this is Agnès, my future wife."

Agnès, busy at the stove, turns around.

"Agnès, this is Marcel, the man who saved my life."

Agnès approaches Marcel and holds out her arms to him.

"We kiss?" asks Agnès.
"We kiss!" replies Marcel.

Marcel gives the flowers to Agnès and she thanks him with a gracious smile.

The three of them sit at the table and talk casually. They start joking and laughing. The ice is broken. Marcel watches Agnès attentively. He finds her pretty. She has beautiful cheeks like Fat John likes. She likes to laugh. That's good, the two friends do, too. It is true she is a little plump but not that much. It doesn't matter, Fat John likes her as she is.

After the traditional Christmas meal of turkey stuffed with cranberries and mashed potatoes, they enjoy a "Bûche de Noel", a delight of lightness, chocolate and sugar prepared by Fat John.

Obviously, Fat John offers a small glass of rum for digestion, and Marcel thinks it's a good time to offer his surprise. He reaches into the inside pocket of his jacket and pulls out a messy stack of papers.

He looks at Agnès and says to her.

"Fat John told me that his love letters never arrived."

"Unfortunately, no." answers Agnès.

"In the trenches, when I saw the beautiful love letters that Fat John wrote, I asked him if I could copy them. I had never written love letters."

Fat John looks at Marcel and can't believe the lies his friend is telling with such poise and ease. But he does not contradict his version of the story.

"I found all these papers in my belongings and I would like to give them to you. They are the words of love from your future husband."

Agnès takes the pile of paper and whispers a little thank you. She looks lovingly at Fat John and starts to read. Marcel and Fat John look at each other and remain silent. Agnès turns the pages and browses through them and the words full of love.

"The time without you is too long. It expands so as not to end. It thickens so as not to move."

She turns a page...

"*Our happy and laughing walks are still and always will be my most beautiful memories. I see again the rays of sun through the yellow leaves of the chestnut trees. I still feel your hand in my hand. And, I always hear your mischievous little laugh.*"

A few pages later...

"*In my dreams, when I can dream, I travel to you. I am in an unknown land, but you are always my destination. It is the only purpose I have. And when I find you, I am finally at peace . I would so love to kiss you.*"

And more....

"*I can no longer keep to myself this heartbeat that overwhelms me and carries me away. I would so much like to share it with you. And I don't want to believe that you don't feel it.*"

A few more pages....

"I get drunk on you, your soul and your smile. My arms call for you to come and snuggle up against me. Again and again. I dream and hope. It's all I can do for now, my love."

"When the war is over and it will end one day, the road to you will be the road of happiness. And it will be an endless road. A road of life."

"Know with all your heart - I love you. But, will you love me back? What if I come back hurt? Will you still love me? And when I grow old, will you still love me?"

The collection of sweet words and love letters goes on and on, and there are still pages and pages. Agnès stops reading and puts everything on the table. She keeps her head down and when she finally looks at Fat John both men see the tears in her eyes.

"My Fat John, your love letters are the most beautiful love letters in the history of love letters."

Fat John's smile gleamed. Agnès gets up and comes to kiss the love of her life.

Marcel, still at the table, looks away and continues to drink his small glass of rum. He hears the lovebirds whispering and thinks it's probably time for him to go.

"I will leave the lovers alone."

Fat John turns around. "Are you sure?"
"Yes, I am sure."
"It's not midnight yet!"

But Marcel is already in the shop and opens the door to the street. Fat John accompanies him outside.

"Marcel, thank you for that big lie."
"Little lie. I just put your words to music."

They shake hands and Marcel puts a finger to his mouth.

"Our lips are sealed."
"Okay, Marcel."

They embrace, wish each other a very Merry Christmas and part ways.

Marcel crosses the street and turns to look at the pastry shop. He wonders if Agnès is going to go back to her parents tonight. He waits two or three minutes and sees the light in the back room go out. He smiles and thinks there will be a wedding soon.

Marcel walks slowly to go back to his room where he will sleep alone. One day soon, he will find a woman to love and who will love him back despite his injuries. He is certain of it.

On the way, he passes close to three churches and all are ringing their bells. It's midnight and it's Christmas. The day when the world makes peace. The day when love on earth joins love in heaven for the happiness of all.

*

Françoise and Louise have finally arrived at their destination and are getting off the tram.

Walking down the street with Louise, Françoise starts talking again.

"It's true Marcel always loved Christmas."
"Yeah, you remember the strange shrubbery he used as a fir tree."

"Yes! Every year, he left town and brought back a shrub from the forest which he planted in a pot in the middle of the living room and put candles around it."

"And Jeanne was decorating the little shrub full of garlands."

"Yeah, it reminded him that he had been through hell, but had a few moments of respite...just a moment of peace...at Christmas."

*
*
*

Epilogue

At the end of the WWI, all the forces counted their dead and arrived at the astronomical figure of 10 million human losses. From here the war became known as "The Great War".

As if death were not satisfied, the Spanish flu invaded the world in March 1918 and killed tens of millions more men and women.

And, as if the madness of men had no limit, twenty years after the First World War, a Second World War is marching rapidly towards the carnage of more than 70 million dead.

Will we ever learn?

On November 11, 2018, one hundred years after the end of WWI, Anita de Hohenberg, the great-granddaughter of François-Ferdinand de Habsbourg, the prince assassinated in Sarajevo and filmmaker Branislav Principe, a descendant of Gavrilo Principe, the Serb nationalist who killed the prince, met in Graz, Austria.

This meeting was very emotional for both of the descendants and was called "The Hands of Peace" by the Austrian and Serbian press.

It is never too late to make peace.
And to make peace, no time is better than Christmas.

*

AFTERWORD - The United States of America in WWI

Almost three years after the beginning of the conflict, on June 13, 1917, General Pershing and Captain Patton landed at Boulogne-sur-Mer with less than two hundred men. In this small port in northern France, they were greeted by a jubilant crowd. They had not yet done anything and they were already heroes.

But why so late?

From the beginning of the conflict, the Americans did not want to hear about a military intervention in Europe. For more than fifty years, American policy had been essentially isolationist and was supported by President Woodrow Wilson.

After the crisis of July 1914 and the beginning of the conflict, President Wilson officially declared on August 19 that America would remain neutral.

Nevertheless, America sends its support to France and England. Food and armaments were transported by ship to Europe much to the irritation of Germany.

In 1915, a British liner was sunk by a German submarine. Following the death of 114 Americans among the 1,198 civilian victims, President Wilson sent a protest to Germany. However, the protest carried no consequences.

Germany did not hesitate to organize terrorist attacks and blow up arms factories on American territory. Still, America remained neutral.

During the presidential election campaign of 1916, Woodrow Wilson repeated his slogan over and over again. *"Thanks to me, America has stayed out of the European conflict."* He was elected for a second term, but the president knew it would be difficult to remain neutral in the face of this war. Neutrality became armed neutrality.

At the beginning of 1917, the American president pleaded for a negotiated peace. At the same time, everyone knew that hundreds of American cargo ships were sailing in the waters of the war. The American irritation increased a notch. Germany decided on a total naval and submarine war!

A few days later, a diplomatic communication between Germany and Mexico was intercepted and deciphered by the secret services. Germany offered financial aid to Mexico to assist them in recapturing the lost territories of Texas, New Mexico and Arizona. This episode will become known in the history books as the "Zimmerman Telegram".

Continuing their attacks, Germany sunk several American merchant ships killing thousands of Americans. This time, American opinion was turned around and President Wilson was supported when he asked for congressional approval to declare war on Germany.

On April 6, 1917, American officially goes to war with Germany.

The compulsory draft is approved and increases the military strength from 200,000 men to 4 million. Only 2 million soldiers will cross the Atlantic.

The war machine was launched and nothing could stop it.

After the arrival of Pershing and Patton with a small contingent of soldiers, things moved quickly. No less than eighteen deep-water ports were identified for the landing of men and equipment. On June 26, 1917, the first ships of a convoy from New York brought in nearly 15,000 men. For several weeks, soldiers arrived daily.

Starting immediately, and for several months afterward, the American soldiers took care of logistics with creation of artificial harbours with floating docks that could accommodate more than twenty ships at a time, construction of dozens of barracks, landing strips and railroads linking all the soldiers' camps.

The French gave a warm welcome to all American soldiers. They had money to spend and were very good customers. Shop owners were happy to see the Americans in their stores. To the women they seemed to be rich....and, who knows, maybe they could even be future husbands.

The agreement between France and America provides for the supply of tanks and artillery of all sizes with shells. In fact, the American army landed in Europe without heavy weaponry. They have only rifles and handguns.

The training of the American soldiers was done by French officers with the help of some industrialists. At the end of October 1917, all the military logistics were ready and early November 1917, the first engagements of the American army began. The new guns, powerful and precise, were a marvel. But the weapon that fascinated most was the Renault FT tank. This armoured vehicle with its overhanging tracks and pivoting turret worked miracles on the battlefield.

The tank crosses the trenches, crushes the barbed wire and breaks the German lines. Every day, new engagements begin. Every week, new battles are won. The Germans retreated, but did not give up yet.

On January 8, 1918, President Wilson presented his fourteen-point peace program and the creation of the League of Nations, the forerunner of the United Nations.

During this time, a general strike of workers began in Germany. But the German army did not disarm and bombed the French capital with the "Paris Gun", a cannon capable of firing shells over 100 miles.

The summer of 1918, the German forces began to run out of steam and finally retreated. The German front line, called "Hindenburg Line", is definitively broken. The Kaiser tried several separate peace deals, country by country, but without success. In addition, anger rumbles in his country. Revolts and strikes multiply and are organized in all major cities in Germany.

On October 29, 1918, the men of the German navy mutinied in Kiel. From that point on, the political, military and revolutionary events accelerated until the abdication of the Kaiser, the proclamation of the Weimar Republic and the signing of the armistice on November 11, 1918.

President Wilson went to Paris to work on the "Treaty of Versailles" which itself was based on Wilson's 14 peace proposals. But, he was quickly marginalized.

After a few weeks of negotiations, he left for Washington DC but not before paying a visit to King Albert I to congratulate him for his bravery during the conflict and to officially invite him to America.

Back in America, President Wilson did not succeed in convincing Congress to ratify the "Treaty of Versailles". America will not enter the "League of Nations". It will take a second world conflict for America to enter the international realm of nations.

*

One last word....and another story....

On July 4, 1917, all over France, America's Independence Day was celebrated by American soldiers, joined by French soldiers, civil authorities and the French citizens.

In Paris, at the Picpus cemetery, all officials made speeches in front of the tomb of a famous marquis. Among them were Colonel Stanton, Commander of the American military mission, General Pershing, Commander of the American expeditionary corps in France, General Joffre, Chief of the French army, Paul Painlevé, French Minister of War, and William Graves Sharp, U.S. Ambassador to France.

Colonel Stanton made a speech that will long be remembered. He made it in honor of "the hero of both worlds":

"I regret that I cannot address the people of France in the beautiful language of their loyal country.

The fact cannot be forgotten that your nation was our friend when America fought for her existence, and when a handful of brave and patriotic men were determined to defend the rights their Creator had given them -- France came to our aid in word and deed.

It would be ingratitude not to remember this, and America will not fail in her obligations.

Therefore, it is with great pride that we embrace the colors in tribute of respect to this citizen of your great Republic, and here and now in the shadow of the illustrious dead, we assure him of our heart and honor to give this war a favorable outcome.

Lafayette, here we are!"

But this is another story ...

of the same author :

- A Small Bed for Two
- Ernest and Solomon
- The Kiss of the Rat

Made in the USA
Columbia, SC
27 September 2023